Child's Play

Easy Art for Preschoolers

Leslie Hamilton

CB
CONTEMPORARY BOOKS

Library of Congress Cataloging-in-Publication Data

Hamilton, Leslie, 1950–   .
    Child's play : easy art for preschoolers / by Leslie Hamilton.
      p.   cm.
    Includes index.
    ISBN 0-8092-3939-9
    1. Art—Study and teaching (Preschool)
LB1140.5.A7H35   1998
372.5'2—dc21   98-36561
                                              CIP

Cover design by Monica Baziuk
Interior design by Hespenheide Design

Published by Contemporary Books
A division of NTC/Contemporary Publishing Group, Inc.
4255 West Touhy Avenue, Lincolnwood (Chicago), Illinois 60646-1975 U.S.A.
Copyright © 1999 by Leslie Hamilton
Printed in the United States of America
International Standard Book Number: 0-8092-3039-9

98 99 00 01 02 03 MV 18 17 16 15 14 13 12 11 10 9 8 7 6 5 4 3 2 1

To Larry, Sarah, and Dave

CONTENTS

● ■ ▲ ● ■ ▲ ● ■ ▲ ● ■ ▲ ● ■ ▲ ● ■ ▲ ● ■ ▲

1

PUTTING THINGS UP
AND TAKING THINGS DOWN

1

2

PLAYING WITH COLOR

5

3

PAPER PLAY
11

Starting Out

More Fun with Paper and Paste

Paper Projects

4

EASY ART GAMES
37

Colors and Shapes

Opposite Art

Hunt Around

5

DRAWING ON PAPER
47

Scribble Away

Rubbings

Tracing

Fun with Chalk

Fun with Drawing

6

PAINTING
77

7

PRINTING
97

8

PLAYING WITH CLAY
115

9

CREATIVE CREATIONS

127

ACKNOWLEDGMENTS

● ■ ▲ ● ■ ▲ ● ■ ▲ ● ■ ▲ ● ■ ▲ ● ■ ▲ ● ■ ▲ ● ■ ▲

Special thanks to Alicita Hamilton, Kathy Harhai, and Betty Bona for their good advice about children and their art, and to Eric Stelter for his hand print and resultant blue hand.

I am grateful to Kara Leverte for her editing expertise, and to Craig Bolt, project editor extraordinaire.

And finally, thank you, Sarah and Dave, for all those wonderful scribbles, drawings, paintings, and sculptures that I have kept and treasured all these many years. They are the inspiration for this book.

A NOTE TO PARENTS
AND CAREGIVERS

●■▲●■▲●■▲●■▲●■▲●■▲●■▲●■▲

Preschoolers are natural artists. Delightfully uninhibited, they instinctively use crayons, paint, paper, and paste in wonderfully creative ways. *Child's Play: Easy Art for Preschoolers* is a collection of simple, open-ended art ideas, games, and activities for you to do with your child, or for older children to do on their own.

There is no right or wrong way to do preschool art. Exploring art should be a fun and relaxing way for your child to learn and grow. Introduce new ideas or projects slowly, taking cues from your child's abilities, interests, and mood. Often, kids are happy to simply repeat certain art techniques over and over again, learning, practicing, and reinforcing their skills each time.

Not all art projects are right for all children. Be sensitive to your child's personal style. Some kids like to get messy and gooey, while others do not. Some young artists love working with lots of bright colors, while others prefer black, white, and shades of gray. Use the symbol system described in the following section, and consider your child's personality and preferences when choosing activities for the day.

CHOOSING PROJECTS FOR YOUR CHILD

● ■ ▲ ● ■ ▲ ● ■ ▲ ● ■ ▲ ● ■ ▲ ● ■ ▲ ● ■ ▲ ● ■ ▲

The symbols below will help you choose appropriate art projects for your child. However, trust your own judgment! You know best when your child is ready to try something more difficult, or when he or she would feel most comfortable practicing familiar skills.

● **Beginner Activity.** For children 2 to 3 years old who are just beginning their coloring, painting, pasting, and scissors skills. These crafts require lots of adult help and supervision, but ask for little in the way of a child's patience.

■ **Intermediate.** Children 3 to 4¹/₂ years old, who have practiced and mastered some art skills, will enjoy spending a little more time on these projects. Adult help and supervision should be nearby, when needed.

▲ **"Professional Artist."** Children 4 to 6 years of age, who are comfortable with a variety of skills, are ready for these more elaborate art activities, projects, and experiments. Often, Professional Artists can manage much of a project on their own. However, the more complicated activities will require adult help.

Most projects are marked with ● ■, ■ ▲, or ● ■ ▲ and appeal to children of mixed ages and abilities.

The caution symbol, !, is a reminder to take extra care and provide close adult supervision.

GETTING STARTED

Most of the projects in this book use art and household supplies you either have in your home right now or can buy at the supermarket. There's no need to buy expensive or fancy materials. Stick to the basics, and pick and choose whatever feels right for your household and your child. Use the list below for suggestions or reminders about art supplies and sources.

Please be sure all materials and supplies are safe and nontoxic! Adult supervision is strongly recommended for the safety of your child!

Making Your Mark. Washable markers are great for young artists because they produce big, bright colors without having to press down very hard. They can color a large space in a short time, are versatile, and work on a wide variety of surfaces. Best of all, they don't break in half if you push too hard. Other ways to make your mark are crayons, pencils, pens, chalk (white, colored, and big sticks of sidewalk chalk for outdoor play), children's liquid paint (poster paint), watercolors, or fingerpaints (homemade or store bought).

All Kinds of Paper. Plain and construction paper are the basics, but think about using newsprint, typing paper, computer paper, tissue paper, freezer paper, shelf paper, brown paper bags, paper plates, napkins, paper towels, recycled gift wrap, junk mail, facial tissues, corrugated cardboard, and poster board.

Sticky Stuff. For sticking things together, you can use clear tape, masking tape, duct tape, colored plastic or cloth tape, paste, glue stick, white glue, and liquid starch.

Scissors. For your child, look for good quality "safety scissors" that cut paper easily, but will not cut skin, hair, or fabric. Have some good, heavyweight scissors for adult use. A few of the crafts call for adults to use a razor knife.

Throwaways and Recyclables. Recycling and creativity go hand-in-hand when you use any of the following: junk mail, coupon sheets, old magazines or catalogs, egg cartons, plastic margarine containers and lids, used gift wrap, cardboard boxes of all shapes and sizes, cardboard tubes from rolls of paper towels or gift wrap, Styrofoam grocery trays, and other recyclable materials.

Household Supplies. Your kitchen is filled with art supplies such as aluminum foil, kitchen utensils, food color, dish detergent, soap, string or yarn, liquid starch, and ingredients for homemade play dough and clay (see Chapter 8).

Work Space. A highchair is the perfect place for very young artists. Tape paper to the highchair tray for easy drawing or painting. Cleanup is simple, and your child can wear a bib or smock to protect clothing.

For older children, cover your work table with a plastic tablecloth, plastic placemats, newspaper, freezer paper, or brown paper grocery bags. For particularly messy projects, you might want to spread newspaper on the floor.

Sometimes your child may enjoy his or her own personal work space. Try making a fast and easy "Box Desk" (see Index).

Smocks. Old shirts make great smocks. If a button-up shirt is unavailable, slit an old pullover up the back. Once your child has it on, fasten the back with a couple of safety pins. Push sleeves above elbows and you're ready to go.

Supply Station. The easier it is to set up and clean up your art supplies, the more often they will be used. Try to find a closet, cabinet, box, or shelves that you and your child can get to easily.

Storage. See Chapter 1, "Putting Things Up and Taking Things Down."

"IT'S A BROWN DOG PLAYING IN MUD," or HOW TO BE A SUPPORTIVE ART CRITIC

● ■ ▲ ● ■ ▲ ● ■ ▲ ● ■ ▲ ● ■ ▲ ● ■ ▲ ● ■ ▲ ● ■ ▲

So what do you say when your child proudly produces a sheet of paper covered completely with thick brown paint? Well, you don't have to go on and on about how much you love it, unless you really *do*. The best approach is to tell the truth in a supportive way: "That's the brownest picture I've ever seen! Way to go!" or "Wow! That brown paint really *does* look like mud! Would you show me where the dog is hiding?"

Some other useful comments to keep in mind are

> "Tell me about it."
> "I like the colors (textures/technique) you used."
> "That picture matches my sweater!"
> "That looks like it took a lot of work. Good job!"
> "Those two colors look good together."
> "I especially like the way you made those dots/wavy lines/spots."
> "Look how you filled the whole page with color! Was that fun?"

Of course, not all artwork is praiseworthy. Sometimes kids aren't in the mood for art. Or they decide to go for quantity over quality, producing stacks of "two-minute masterpieces." And some children might want to see how you'll react to something he or she thinks is really awful. You might want to ask questions like, "How do you feel about this picture?" or "What's your favorite part of this painting?" If you sense that your child's art session is heading downhill, wrap it up and go on to something else.

1
PUTTING THINGS UP
AND TAKING THINGS DOWN

It's a good idea to have several display or storage strategies for finished artwork. Ask your child, "Should we put this picture up? Where? What should we take down to make room?" Also, "Recycled Art Collage" (see page 23) is a fun way to reuse, recycle, and use up earlier masterpieces.

● ■ ▲ INSTANT PICTURE FRAME

This is a way to honor a really special paper creation. Not all drawings or paintings need to be framed. Save this activity for those extra special artworks before taping them to the refrigerator or kitchen cupboards.

You need:
➡ Beautiful paper art creation
➡ Contrasting color construction paper (slightly larger than artwork)
➡ Clear tape

Child does: Chooses construction paper that looks best with artwork.

You and child do: Use loops of tape to attach artwork to a larger piece of construction paper, so that a 1–1$^{1}/_{2}$ inch border is created. You may want to slightly trim the edges of the artwork. (Using loops of clear tape makes it easy to eventually remove the artwork and reuse the construction paper.)

● ■ ▲ PICTURES ON A LINE

You need:
- ➡ Clothesline or sturdy string
- ➡ Clothespins

You and child do: Figure out the best place to hang a clothesline in child's bedroom or playroom. Clothesline should extend the length of the room, if possible, but be high enough to be out of reach and out of the way.

Child does: Decides which pictures should be hung.

You do: Attach artwork with clothespins. As space on clothesline gets used up, let child decide what comes down to make room for new pictures.

● ■ ▲ PORTFOLIO

This is a quick and easy way to create a storage place for flat artwork. It also comes in handy as a safe place to keep a "work-in-progress."

You need:
- ➡ One piece of poster board, colored or white
- ➡ Masking tape, duct tape, packaging tape, or colored plastic tape
- ➡ Crayons or markers
- ➡ Stickers (optional)

You and child do: Fold poster board in half, as shown. Seal side edges with tape, and decorate front and back of portfolio with markers, crayons, or stickers.

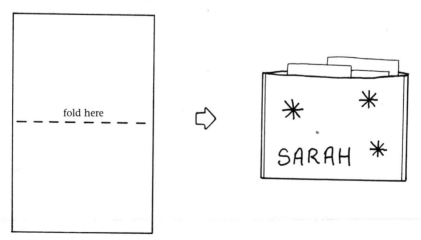

fold here

SARAH

■ ▲ STORAGE BOX

Use this storage box to store lightweight paper art.

You need: ➡ Medium-size, sturdy cardboard box
➡ A second box, slightly larger than the first
➡ Sharp scissors or razor knife
➡ Yardstick
➡ Pencil
➡ Masking tape
➡ Poster paints, prepasted wallpaper scraps, or recycled gift wrap (optional)
➡ White glue (optional)

You do: Cut top flaps off the smaller of the two boxes. If desired, decorate the outside of the box with paints, wallpaper scraps, or glued-on gift wrap. Lay the box on its side, divide the side into thirds, and mark with pencil. Repeat on opposite side (1).

! Use the razor knife or scissors to cut slits in the sides of the box, as shown, stopping about one inch from the back of the box (2). Cut panels from the larger box, for shelves.

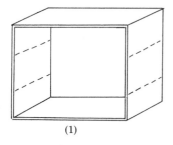 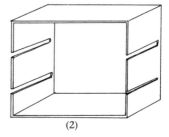

(1)   (2)

You and child do: Slide cardboard panels into slits to make shelves (3). Secure shelves with tape, if necessary.

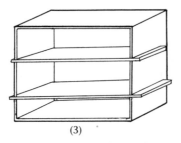

(3)

2
PLAYING WITH COLOR

● ■ ▲ COLOR SWIRLS

You need:
→ Clear glass jar or drinking glass
→ Food color (available in grocery stores)
→ Water
→ Spoon and fork

You and child do:
Fill glass with cold water. As child watches from the side, add one or two drops of food color to the water. Watch as the color swirls through the water.

Pour out the water, rinse and refill the glass. This time, use the spoon to stir the water in a circular motion. Remove the spoon and, as child watches from side, add a drop or two of color. Try the experiment again, this time, stirring back and forth with the fork.

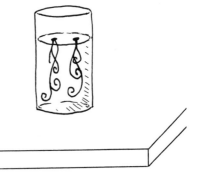

● ■ ▲ FOOD COLOR MIXERS

You need:
→ Clear glass jar or drinking glass
→ Food colors (red, yellow, and blue)
→ Water
→ Spoon

You and child do:
Fill glass with water. Ask your child to count as you slowly add five drops of blue food color. Stir. Now add five drops of yellow food color. Stir. Ask your child to tell you what has happened to the water!

Rinse the glass and refill with clean water. Repeat the procedure above, this time using red and yellow food color. Repeat, using blue and red. Ask your child to choose the colors to mix.

Encourage older children to guess what color certain combinations will produce. Then mix the colors to see if their guess is correct.

You need:
➡ Short, clear glass jars or drinking glasses (approximately 8-ounce size)
➡ Measuring cup
➡ Measuring spoon
➡ Spoon for stirring
➡ Food colors
➡ Household bleach
➡ Water

❗ Note of caution:
This activity uses bleach. Adult supervision is necessary at all times. Protect children, work surface, and clothing from contact with bleach.

You and child do:
Fill one glass with $1/2$ cup water. Add one drop green food color to water. Stir.

You do:
Add $1/4$ teaspoon bleach to green water.

You and child do:
Stir solution and observe surprising results!
   Repeat procedure, mixing one drop yellow food color and $1/4$ teaspoon bleach.
   Repeat procedure mixing one drop blue food color and $1/4$ teaspoon bleach.

Older child variations:
• Older children may want to make more complicated mixes. Add one drop of blue and one drop of yellow to $1/2$ cup water. Stir. Add 1 teaspoon bleach and stir again. Set this mixture aside for fifteen minutes, and check to see what happens!
• Or, try adding one drop red food color and one drop green to $1/2$ cup water, and then adding one teaspoon bleach. Stir.
• Try adding one drop each of red, blue, green, and yellow to $1/2$ cup water. Then add 1 teaspoon bleach. Stir.

You need:
- ➡ Food colors (especially red, blue, and yellow)
- ➡ Aluminum foil
- ➡ White paper towels
- ➡ Water
- ➡ Plastic medicine cup or other small cup
- ➡ Cookie sheet (optional)

You and child do: Lay a 14-inch sheet of aluminum foil on your work surface, and cover with a paper towel. Drip food colors, one drop at a time, onto the paper towel. Let child decide which colors to use and where the drops should go. When you have about 8 to 12 drips, ask child to pour about ½ teaspoon of water over each spot of color. (A small plastic medicine cup is perfect for this.) Watch as the colors spread and blend. When colors are blended to child's satisfaction, set foil and paper aside to dry.

Note: For faster drying, lay paper on a cooling rack or hang from a line using clothespins.

Cookie sheet variation: Lay a dry paper towel in a cookie sheet. Drip food colors, one drop at a time, onto the paper towel. You'll want to use between 15 and 20 drops of color. Ask your child to pour about ¼ cup of water over the paper towel. Tip the cookie sheet from side to side and watch as colors blend. Tip the cookie sheet over the sink and drain off excess colored water. (Water drains best from a *corner* of the paper towel.)

! Set aside to dry, or dry in 200° F oven for about 15 minutes, *watching carefully.*

■ ▲ PAINT MIXERS

You need:
➡ White plastic lids from margarine tubs, large yogurt tubs, etc.
➡ Masking tape
➡ Blue, red, and yellow liquid paint
➡ Paintbrushes or cotton swabs
➡ Paper towels

You do:
Use two or three loops of tape to secure the flat side of the margarine lid to the work surface.

You and child do:
At first, offer child only one color to apply to margarine lid. Many children prefer to use their fingers instead of a brush. Eventually, add a dab of a second color and watch as child smears colors together to create a new color. Clean the margarine lid with a damp paper towel, and start again, this time with two different colors. Experiment with different color combinations. If white or black paint is available, use them to lighten or darken the colors.

Note:
If child wishes to keep a margarine lid painting, allow painting to dry and attach to refrigerator door with loops of masking tape.

9

You need:
➡ Picture books
➡ Selection of child's drawings or paintings
➡ Paper and a selection of paints, crayons, or markers (optional)

You and child do:
Talk to your child about how colors can make people feel. Some colors (reds, oranges, yellows) look warm, while other colors (blues, greens, violets) look cool. Talk about how color can express emotions like happiness, peace, sadness, or anger.

Look around the room and ask your child about the colors around you. Are they happy or sad? Loud or quiet? Exciting or restful? Do some colors make you sleepy while other colors wake you up? Look through a picture book and talk about how the colors help a picture tell its story. Look at some of your child's old drawings or paintings, and talk about how the colors make you feel.

Child does:
Draws or paints a picture, deciding if it's happy, sad, excited, sleepy, etc.

3
PAPER PLAY

STARTING OUT

● RIP IT!

You need: ➡ A large supply of all sorts of scrap paper (newspapers, magazines, junk mail, catalogs, etc.)

You and child do: The simple act of tearing paper is great fun for young children. Even the sound is entertaining, especially when accompanied by a child saying, "Riiippp!" Very young children may appreciate some help with early tearing attempts. Make small tears about an inch or two apart in the top of a page of paper, creating a series of tabs. Then, while you hold the paper, show your child how to grasp the first tab and pull, tearing off a strip of paper.

Encourage your child to tear a page into one or two *big* pieces. Then tear a page into many *tiny* pieces.

As you tear, your child may notice that pages tear in a relatively straight line in one direction, but tear unevenly in the other direction. Experiment with different paper to see which direction is most fun for tearing.

Note: Save your colorful paper scraps to use in other projects, such as "Paper and Paste."

● CUT IT!

A toddler activity to practice scissors skills.

You need:
- → Good quality, children's safety scissors (Make sure they really cut.)
- → Junk mail, coupon pages from Sunday paper, old magazines

You and child do:
With child on your lap, demonstrate how to hold scissors and make them cut. Then, *you* hold the paper, while child practices scissors skills, as follows:
1. You hold the paper as child cuts randomly.
2. You hold the paper as child tries to cut along a straight line.
3. You hold the paper as child cuts a curved line and eventually a circle. You can help by gently turning the paper as child cuts.
4. Child holds paper while you cut. Child can maneuver paper and control the shape of the finished product.

Note:
Save your colorful paper scraps to use in other projects.

● ■ PAPER AND PASTE

You need:
- → Bowl, tray, or basket of torn-up or cut-up scraps of colorful paper
- → Paste, glue stick, or white glue
- → Background paper (a sheet of white or construction paper)

Notes:
Use paper scraps from "Rip It!" and "Cut It!" or keep a supply of colorful scraps on hand. Try to have scraps of all different sizes and shapes.

Plain white paste or glue, available at grocery stores, is fine for paper projects. Just be sure ingredients are nontoxic, and that the paste isn't dried out. Children can choose between applying paste with an applicator, Popsicle stick, or fingers. If you are using white glue, pour a small amount into a yogurt or margarine lid, and children can dip fingers, cotton swabs, or bits of paper into it. (You may want to secure the lid to the work surface with a loop or two of masking tape.) Most young children will need help applying paste at first.

Child does: Pastes scraps to larger sheet of paper in a free-form, random pattern. Pasting techniques vary widely: some children will quickly cover the page with large scraps of paper, while others painstakingly place small scraps here and there. Some children will slather scraps with paste, while others will use paste sparingly. Some children will concentrate on one or two colors, while others will try to use all the colors. And some children will make stacks of scraps, pasting one scrap on top of another.

**You and
child do:**

Try some of the following experiments and then make up some of your own:

- Use only black and white scraps on a colored background.

- Use only two colors of scraps.
- Use only tiny scraps.
- Make a collage using exactly five scraps. Then try exactly ten scraps.

- Make a collage where scraps are all separate. Then make a collage where scraps are all touching.

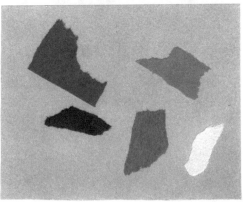

● ■ ▲ TORN PAPER COLLAGE

You need:
→ Construction paper (many colors)
→ Background paper or cardboard
→ Paste, white glue, or glue stick

Child does: Chooses colors of paper to work with, and tears paper into shapes. Encourage your child to create interesting and different shapes. Talk about big and little, long and short, circles, squares, triangles, strips, etc. Child pastes or glues shapes to sheet of paper.

Variations: Use newspaper or magazine scraps.
Use paper from around the house (paper towels, junk mail, used gift wrap).

You need: ➡ Construction paper (many colors)
➡ Background paper or cardboard
➡ Safety scissors
➡ Paste, white glue, or glue stick

You and child do: Children still working on their scissors skills will need help cutting shapes for their collage. You and your child can sit together and work on cutting shapes of varying size, shape, and color. Toddlers may enjoy cutting wide strips and little bits, while you cut circles, triangles, and squares.

Child does: Pastes or glues shapes to sheet of paper.

Idea: Compare a "Torn Paper Collage" and a "Cut Paper Collage" with your child. Talk about how they are different (edges, shapes, patterns) and how they are the same (colors, shapes). Ask your child which kind of collage he or she likes best and why.

17

■ ▲ TAKE A CLOSER LOOK—
TEARING AND CUTTING

Looking at common things through a magnifying glass shows children how the ordinary can look extraordinary—a new way to look at the world.

You need:
- Large magnifying glass (available at drug stores)
- Different kinds of paper (newspaper, notebook paper, construction paper, tissue paper, brown paper bags, etc.)
- Scissors

Child does: With each type of paper, child tears a piece and cuts a piece to create two different types of edges.

You and child do: Examine the cut and torn edges of paper with the magnifying glass. Talk about how clean and smooth the cut edges are, compared to the rough, torn edges. Child will discover that paper is made up of tiny fibers!

18

MORE FUN WITH PAPER AND PASTE

Pasting paper or objects to a background creates the art form called "collage," a wonderful opportunity for creativity and freedom. Experiment with different kinds of paper: newspaper, magazines, paper towels, construction paper, gift wrap, tissue paper, foil, etc. You can also think about different background types, shapes, sizes, and colors, using cardboard, poster board, or construction paper. A white paper plate makes a handy background for a quick and portable collage.

See Chapter 9, "Creative Creations," for some three-dimensional collage ideas.

● ■ ▲ ADD-ON COLLAGE

You need:
→ Construction paper scraps (many colors)
→ Background paper or cardboard
→ Safety scissors
→ Paste, white glue, or glue stick

● Toddler variation: Take turns pasting torn or cut scraps to background paper. Depending on the types of scraps, you might say as you paste, "I'm putting a little blue scrap of paper right here." Then child can say, "I'm adding on a big red piece." Or you might use precut shapes: "I'm putting down a yellow square." "Well, I'm putting down a green circle." Change the game by using different vocabulary such as *next to* or *under* and *over*.

■ ▲ Older child variation: Cut out paper pieces that resemble familiar objects and take turns pasting them to a background to create a scene. For instance, child can paste down a wide brown strip as a tree trunk, and you can add a big green circle for the leaves. Or you can paste down a square for a house, and your child can add a triangle for a roof. Then you can add squares for windows, as your child adds a yellow circle for the sun. Older children may want to add more details to the collage such as small red circles for apples on the tree. (See illustration on next page.)

19

■ ▲ TORN TISSUE COLLAGE

You need:
➡ Colored tissue paper (two colors)
➡ White paper for background
➡ White glue
➡ Water
➡ Small bowl
➡ Tablespoon
➡ Paintbrush (soft)

You do:
Pour 1 tablespoon of glue into a small bowl and add 1 tablespoon of water, mixing with the paintbrush until smooth.

You and child do:
Tear colored tissue paper into different sizes and shapes. Pieces should be anywhere from 1 to 2 inches across, and you will need about 15 pieces of each color.

Glue the tissue pieces to the white paper in a random pattern, overlapping colors. The easiest way to do this is to paint sections of the white paper with the glue solution, and lay the tissue pieces down. When the collage is finished, paint over the entire surface with a thin layer of glue solution.

!
Allow collage to either air dry or dry it in the microwave for about 1 minute on High, *watching carefully.* The finish will be glossy.

Torn Tissue Collage

■ ▲ MOSAIC

You need:
→ Construction paper (many colors)
→ Background paper
→ Scissors
→ Markers or crayons
→ White glue, paste, or glue stick

Child does: Draws a simple line drawing on background paper. Drawing should have lots of open space to be filled with paper pieces.

21

You and child do: Tear or cut construction paper into small pieces. Spread a thin layer of glue or paste over a small section of the picture and fill in with paper pieces. Repeat for other sections of the drawing, until the entire paper is covered.

Note: Children may run out of energy before the entire page is covered with paper pieces. Either think of this as a two- or three-day craft, or just consider the partially-covered mosaic complete!

Travel Mosaic: If your child enjoys playing with adhesive stickers, buy a package of colorful adhesive labels (circles or rectangles) and use these to make a small mosaic. A white paper plate is an easy and convenient background for your line drawing. This is a nice travel craft since it eliminates the need for glue and loose pieces of paper.

■ ▲ RECYCLED ART COLLAGE

This is a great way to use up old drawings and paintings.

You need:
➡ Collection of child's old drawings or paintings
➡ Scissors
➡ Large piece of background paper
➡ Glue, paste, or glue stick
➡ Markers, crayons, or poster paints (optional)

Child does: Decides which drawings or paintings to cut up, and then decides which figures or designs to cut out for projects.

You and child do: Either cut free-form shapes or individual figures and designs from child's drawings or paintings. Glue or paste the cutouts to the background paper to create a colorful collage. For more elaborate techniques, try the following ideas.

Ideas: *Show It Off.* Glue the cutouts to the background paper. Then use black marker or crayon to outline each paper shape.

Mosaic. Use a collection of cut-out shapes to make a "Mosaic" (see page 21).

Multimedia Mural. Older children can cut out recognizable objects in their pictures (people, house, car, animals, trees, rainbow, sun, clouds, etc.). Glue the cutouts to background paper and then use crayons, markers, or paints to fill the background with new art. Paint a blue sky or green grass. Draw a fence around a cut-out house or draw a funny hat and a big dog for a cut-out person. Draw a pot of gold or a garden of flowers at the end of a cut-out rainbow.

Group Project. Each child chooses a painting or drawing to cut up and then contributes one or more cutouts for a cooperative collage or mural.

■ ▲ COLLAGE OF HOLES

You need:
➡ Small scraps of colorful paper (This is a great way to use up construction paper odds and ends.)
➡ Background paper
➡ Scissors (optional)
➡ Paste, white glue, or glue stick

You and child do:
Help your child fold small scraps of paper in half or in quarters and tear or cut as shown to create a hole.

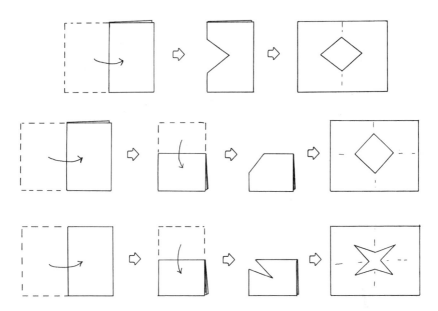

Supply child with paper scraps of different sizes, shapes, and colors, and create a collection of holes. Paste or glue holes to background paper, overlapping holes if desired.

▲ Older   Glue white "Paper Snowflakes" (page 36) to a black
child   paper background for a pretty winter scene. See "Fold
variations: and Cut," page 32.

■ ▲ MONTAGE

A montage is a collage made from many pictures or parts of pictures.

You need:
→ Lots of old magazines with colorful pictures
→ Scissors
→ Background paper
→ Paste, white glue, or glue stick

You and   Let your child choose the magazine pictures to cut out. It
child do: may work best for child to roughly cut out a picture, and
                 you can do the more detailed cutting.

                 Paste or glue pictures to background paper, overlap-
                 ping pictures as desired. Try to cover most or all of the
                 background paper.

Ideas: *Make a Scene.* If you have only a few pictures, your child
                can draw a simple background scene with markers and
                then cut out and glue on animals, people, or objects to
                populate the scene.

Choose a Theme. Child chooses a particular theme for the montage such as sports, animals, favorite foods, cars and boats, or ballet.

Mystery Person. Cut out different parts of different people and paste them together to make a new and amazing person.

Home Sweet Home. Draw a big picture of a house and furnish it with pictures of furniture, people, etc. For a fun and funny project, furnish the house with silly and unrealistic objects. Paste cows in the living room, upside-down tables hanging from ceilings, or a giant banana in the kitchen.

PAPER PROJECTS

● ■ ▲ PAPER CHAIN

You need:
➡ A collection of paper strips, $^3/_4$ inch wide and 6 inches long
➡ Clear tape, paste, or glue stick

You and child do: Show child how to put tape or paste on one end of a paper strip, and then make a loop of paper. Take a second paper strip, thread it through the first loop, and paste or tape it into a loop. Repeat until paper chain is as long as child wants.

● Toddler variation: An easier way to make a paper chain is to make a collection of paper loops first and then attach the connector loops afterward, with adult help.

■ ▲ WEAVING PAPER

You need: ➡ Two pieces of construction paper (contrasting colors are best)
➡ Markers or crayons
➡ Scissors
➡ Clear tape, paste, or glue stick

You do: Fold one sheet of paper in half, as shown, and draw cutting lines about 1 inch apart (1).

You and child do: Cut or tear strips of paper, about $3/4$ to 1 inch wide and 9 to 10 inches long, from the second piece of paper.

Help child cut folded paper along cutting lines. Open paper up to reveal slits (2).

Weave the first strip of paper *over and under* the slits, securing ends with tape or paste. Then weave the second paper strip *under and over* the slits, as shown. Repeat until you run out of room (3).

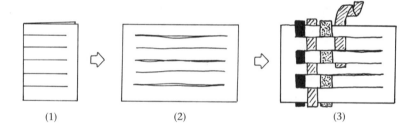

(1)   (2)   (3)

● *Note for beginning weavers*: Less than perfect results are completely acceptable! The "over-under" aspect of weaving is difficult at first, and the idea of alternating over-under with under-over is even more advanced. Your child will catch on eventually.

▲ WEAVING PAPER HEARTS

You need: ➡ Two 3 × 5-inch pieces of construction paper (contrasting colors)
➡ Pencil, marker, or crayon
➡ Ruler
➡ Scissors
➡ Paste, glue stick, or clear tape

You do: Draw the pattern in Figure (1) on one piece of construction paper. Place the two pieces of paper together and cut out the shape. Then cut two 3¼-inch slits, as shown, through both shapes (2).

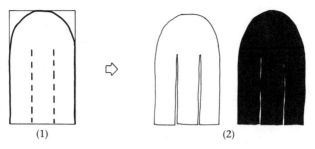

(1)   (2)

You and child do: Place the light-colored shape over the dark shape, as shown (3).

Weave the top light strip over, under, and then over the dark strips (4). Then weave the second light strip under, over, and under the dark strips (5).

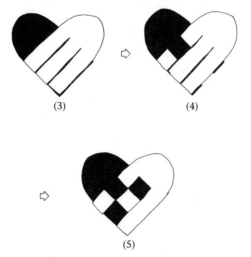

(3)   (4)

(5)

Finally, weave the third light strip over, under, and over the dark strips (6). Paste or tape strip ends.

(6)

You need: ➡ Two like-size strips of paper, one dark and one light
(Strips should be at least 12 inches long.)
➡ Scissors
➡ Clear tape
➡ Markers, crayons, or pencil

You and
child do: Position strips of paper as illustrated in Figure (1), and
tape together on the bottom.

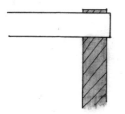

(1)

Fold the dark strip up and over the light strip, as
shown (2).
Fold the light strip to the right, over the dark strip (3).

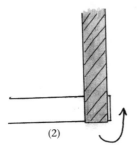

(2)

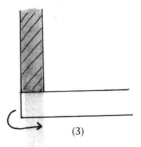

(3)

Fold the dark strip down, over the light strip (4).
Fold the light strip left, over the dark strip (5).

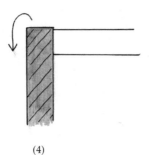

(4)

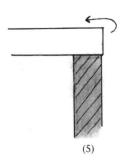

(5)

Continue folding until strips are used up. Tape ends, and pull gently to open caterpillar. Cut a small circle for a head, and decorate with a face. Tape to one end of the caterpillar with a loop of tape (6).

(6)

■ ▲ PAPER BASKET

You need:
- ➡ Square piece of paper (any size)
- ➡ Scissors
- ➡ Clear tape
- ➡ Markers or crayons (optional)

You and child do: Fold paper in half (1). Fold in half again (2). Unfold paper to reveal three fold lines (3).

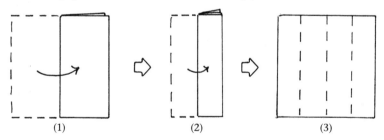

(1) (2) (3)

Fold paper in half in other direction (4). Fold in half again (5). Unfold paper to reveal fold lines (6).

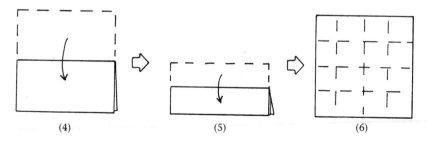

(4) (5) (6)

Cut along fold lines, as shown in Figure (7), to create tabs A, B, C, and D. Bring the edges of tabs A and B together and tape. Bring edges of C and D together and tape (8).

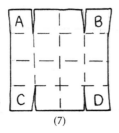

(7)

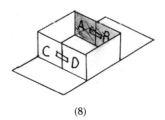

(8)

Fold outer flaps up and tape as shown (9). If desired, add a paper handle and decorate with markers or crayons.

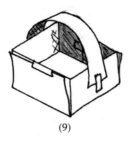

(9)

■ ▲ FOLD AND CUT

This simple activity is a fun way to discover how to cut one shape to produce another.

You need:
➡ Paper
➡ Marker, crayon, or pencil
➡ Scissors
➡ Construction paper (optional)
➡ Paste, white glue, or glue stick

You and child do:
Fold paper in half. Draw a triangle along the folded edge, as shown (1). Cut along triangle cutting lines and unfold paper to produce triangle- or diamond-shaped paper and space (2).

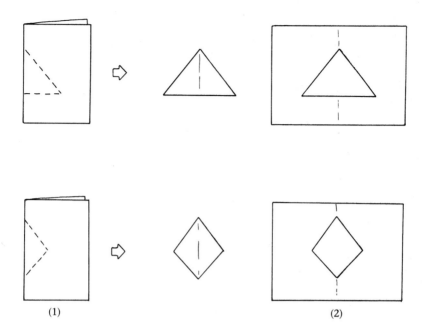

Experiment by drawing and cutting different patterns to produce a circle, rectangle, triangle, or heart. Before you unfold the paper, ask your child to guess what the shape will be.

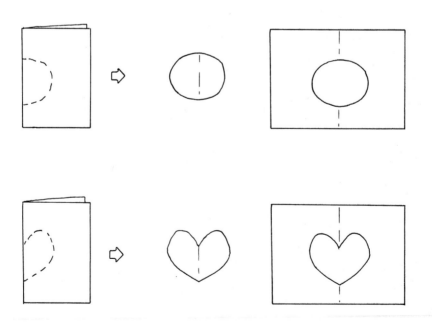

Child may want to paste or glue shapes or cut-out portion of paper on construction paper.

▲ Older child variations:
- Try creating and cutting out more complicated patterns: certain numbers or letters of the alphabet, a flower, or a butterfly.

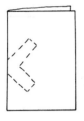   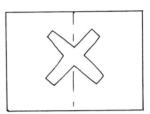

   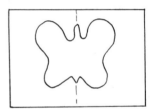

- Try using the original paper as a stencil for "Making Simple Stencils" (page 91) or as a part of a "Collage of Holes" (page 24).
- Fold paper in quarters, cut along folded edges, and unfold.
- See "Giant Paper Dolls" and "Paper Snowflake" (next).

■ ▲ GIANT PAPER DOLLS

Giant-size paper dolls are easier for little hands to cut out and decorate. They make a fun wall decoration.

You need:
- ➡ A large rectangular piece of lightweight paper
- ➡ Markers or crayons
- ➡ Scissors
- ➡ Paper clips (optional)

You and child do: Fold paper in half (1). Fold in half again (2). Fold in half again (3).

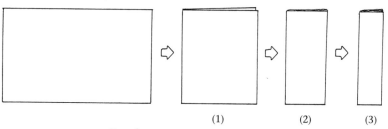

(1)   (2)   (3)

You do:

Draw half shape of doll on *folded edge* of paper, as shown. Center of head should be at fold, and arms and legs must extend all the way to the opposite edge (4). If child will be cutting out doll shape, you may want to secure some of the edges with paper clips, to keep paper from slipping.

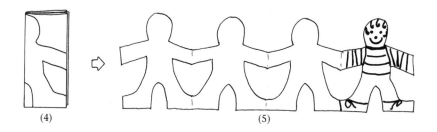

(4)   (5)

You and child do: Cut along cutting lines, through all layers of paper (5). Unfold.

Note: If dolls fall apart at this point, try again, making sure that half-doll shape is on the big folded edge and that arms and legs extend *all the way to the opposite edges.*

Child does: Uses markers or crayons to decorate dolls with faces, hair, clothes, and accessories (5).

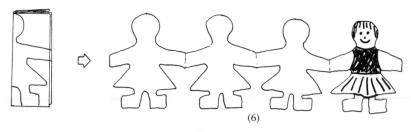

(6)

Note: Follow the pattern in Figure (6) to create paper dolls wearing skirts rather than pants.

▲ PAPER SNOWFLAKE

You need:
- ➡ Square piece of lightweight, white paper (Paper napkins work well.)
- ➡ Scissors
- ➡ Construction paper (optional)
- ➡ Paste, white glue, or clear tape (optional)

You and child do: Fold paper in half (1). Fold in half downward and label corners as shown (2). Fold in half diagonally, so that corner B meets corner D (3). Use scissors to round corner

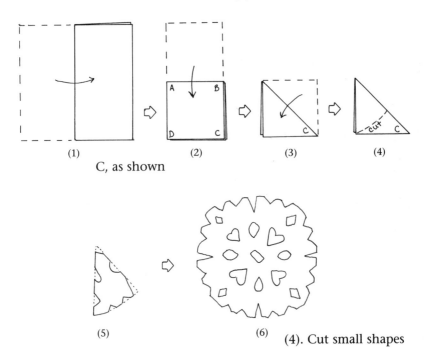

C, as shown

(4). Cut small shapes out of all three edges (5). Unfold to reveal snowflake (6)! If desired, tape, glue, or paste snowflake to contrasting color construction paper.

4

EASY ART GAMES

The best kind of art experience for your child is freestyle art. When children are encouraged to experiment on their own, their imagination and creativity soar. But sometimes you may want a more structured or interactive art experience, or just some quick and easy entertainment.

The following games are fun to play at home, in waiting rooms, in a restaurant, or during an airplane ride. All you need is markers or crayons and blank paper. To keep the mood playful and fun, be sure to choose a game that is well within or below your child's abilities. Rules can easily be changed to suit your child's mood or skills.

COLORS AND SHAPES

● ■ SPOT THE DOT

Using anywhere from two to eight different colors, draw dots all over a piece of white paper. Draw a small number of colors and dots for toddlers, while older children may want more of a challenge. Then ask your child:

"Do you see a red dot? Can you put your finger on it? Good! Now, can you put your finger on a green dot? Can you find another green dot? Can you put your finger on that one?" Older children may want to count or circle the dots as they find them.

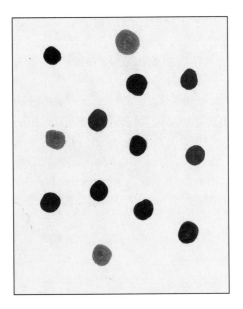

● ■ ▲ MARK IT UP!

Using anywhere from two to eight markers or crayons, ask your child to follow your simple directions:

"Draw a red dot."
"Draw a blue line."
"Which is the purple crayon?"
"Can you draw a purple line that touches the blue line?"

■ ▲ COUNT, COLOR, AND DRAW

Work with fewer colors when playing this game, since counting adds a degree of difficulty and challenge. Ask your child to do the following:

> "Draw two blue dots."
> "Draw three red dots."
> "Draw one orange dot and two green ones."

● ■ ▲ WHERE'S THE SQUARE?

Using one, two, or three different colors, draw a selection of shapes on a piece of paper. Then ask your child questions like these:

> "Do you see a square?"
> "Can you put your finger in the circle?"
> "Where is the orange triangle?"
> "Where is the blue triangle?"

Ask your child to follow directions like these:

"Draw three green circles."

"Draw two blue squares."

"Draw one red circle and one blue circle."

"Draw one green square and two red circles."

"Draw one blue circle, one red square, and one orange triangle."

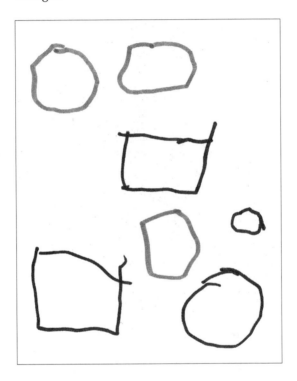

OPPOSITE ART

■ ▲ INSIDE—OUTSIDE

Draw a circle on a piece of paper. Then ask your child to "draw a green dot inside the circle." Then ask your child to "draw a red dot outside of the circle." If your child wants more of a challenge, draw a blue square, with instructions to "draw two red dots outside the square and one green dot inside the square."

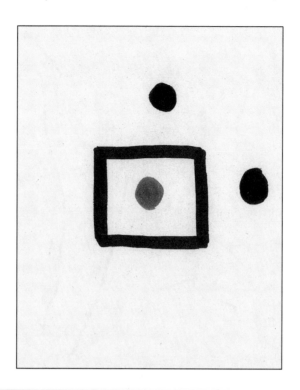

Ask your child to follow these directions, offering help as needed:

> "Draw a red line across the page."
> "Start at the top of the page and draw a blue line down to the bottom."
> "Start at the bottom of the page and draw a green line up to the top." (This is harder.)
> "Draw a yellow line across the bottom of the page."
> "Draw a purple line across the top of the page."

■ ▲ SHORT AND LONG

Ask your child to do the following, offering help as needed:

> "Draw a short black line. Draw a long black line."
> "Draw a short yellow line. Draw a long red line."
> "Draw a long blue line with a short blue line next to it."
> "Draw a long green line. Now draw a short black line across the long green line." (See next page.)

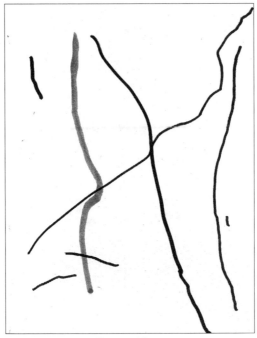

Short and Long

▲ WIGGLY AND STRAIGHT

Ask your child to do the following, offering help as needed:

"Draw a straight blue line. Now draw a wiggly blue line."
"Draw a wiggly green line. Now draw two straight red lines."
"Draw a straight yellow line. Now draw a wiggly blue line on top of it."

▲ LITTLE AND BIG

Ask your child to do the following, offering help as needed:

"Draw a big red square. Now draw a little red square."
"Draw a little blue circle. Now draw a big green circle."
"Draw a big red circle. Now draw a little blue square. "
"Draw a big blue circle. Now draw a little red square inside it."
"Draw a little green square. Now draw a big blue circle around it."

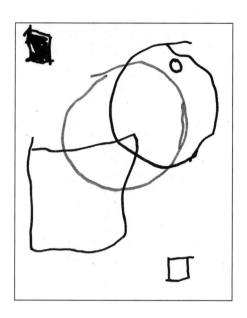

●■▲ HARD AND SOFT

This is a nice use for all those stubby, broken crayons. Ask your child to "push hard with your crayon to make a dark scribble. Now draw softly with your crayon to make a light scribble." As child continues to draw a scribble picture, you can alternate commands: "Hard! Soft! Now hard again! Now soft!"

HUNT AROUND

These easy games are fun to play indoors or out and work especially well in waiting rooms or while traveling.

●■▲ COLOR HUNT

Ask your child to look around, searching with eyes only:

> "Find something brown."
> "Find something blue."
> "Find something the same color as your sweater."
> "Find something light green."
> "Find something dark green."

■▲ SHAPE HUNT

Outdoors, natural shapes often come as surprises: a knothole in a tree, a perfectly square or round pebble, a triangular chip of ice. Also, look for squares on the sidewalk, rectangular bricks, circular clocks, triangular rooftops. Indoors, shapes are everywhere:

- *Circles:* buttons, clocks, banana slices, drinking cups, plates, doorknobs
- *Squares and rectangles:* books, tabletops, windows, dresser drawers, picture frames, paper
- *Triangles:* Triangles are a bit tricky to find. Look for lamp shades, building blocks, puzzle pieces, designs on food boxes or magazine covers, or grapefruit sections.

● ■ ▲ SIZE HUNT

For very young children, simply ask them to point to something *very big*, and then find something very small. You may want to elaborate from there with questions like these:

> "Who is a big person?"
> "Who is a little person?"
> "Can you give me the big teddy bear? Can you bring me the little teddy bear?"
> "Can you find a leaf that is bigger than the one I have?"
> "Now can you find a leaf that is smaller than the one I have?"

● ■ ▲ HUNT AND TOUCH

It's fun to explore your environment using the sense of touch. Ask your child to hunt for something rough and then something smooth, something dry and something wet, something soft and something hard. Talk about how some words *sound* like how they *feel*: fuzzy, slick, rough, scratchy. Talk about how some objects *look* the way they feel: a soft pillow, scratchy sandpaper, smooth glass, a fluffy blanket.

5

DRAWING ON PAPER

Your child's highchair is a perfect location for early works of art. Use masking tape to secure paper to the highchair tray. Offer your toddler one or two crayons at a time, and don't worry if enthusiastic drawing goes off the page. For older children, taping paper to a plastic placemat protects the work surface and makes drawing projects portable. When drawings are finished, peel tape from work surface and fold the tape over to create an instant picture frame.

SCRIBBLE AWAY

Early attempts with crayons or markers will be random scribbles and marks: some on paper, some on the work surface, and some on the child. Projects will take only a few minutes, as long as your child is interested. Over the months and years, your child's drawings will reflect development of large muscle control, eye-hand coordination, and fine-motor skills. Drawings will feature larger, stronger lines that will eventually become curves, ovals, circles, and other shapes. Children start experimenting with straight lines too, drawing up and down, across, long and short, off the paper and on. And then, one day, your child announces, "It's a bunny!" and it is!

● ■ FIRST DRAWINGS

You need: ➡ Crayons, washable markers, or pencil
          ➡ Paper (taped to work surface)

You do: Offer very young children only one or two crayons or markers. Some children prefer to work in one color, or in pencil.

Child does: Experiments with drawing, making random, free-form marks and scribbles on paper.

age 2   age 2½   age 3

Variations: • When your child seems comfortable with scribble pictures, think about offering different textures to draw on. Try chalk scribbles on the driveway or sidewalk; crayon scribbles on corrugated cardboard; or washable markers on aluminum foil (this is messy but fun).

- Older children may want to color in some of the spaces in their scribble pictures.

See also: "Stained Glass Pictures" (page 50) and "Crayon Resist" (page 88).

● ■ ▲ CLOSED-EYES DRAWING

You need: ➡ Crayons or markers
➡ Paper taped to work surface

You and child do: After your child has made one or two drawings, suggest a "Closed-Eyes Drawing." Ask child to choose a color and then close his or her eyes and draw. Continue the activity, changing colors if desired, until your child thinks the drawing is finished. Then compare it with the "open-eyes" drawings to see the differences.

▲ Variation: Older children may want to try a "Closed-Eyes Drawing" of a face or a particular object. Here are two ways to try this:

- With paper taped to work surface, child draws as usual, guessing where features and details should go. Some children place their free hand on the paper, to use as a location guide. It rarely works, and the resulting pictures are fun and funny.
- Suggest that your child use one color only, and try not to lift the crayon, marker, or pencil from the paper as he or she draws.

● ■ ▲ DRAW TO MUSIC

This is a fun activity for adults to do with children. Talk about and compare the feelings you get from the music with those of your child.

You need: ➡ Crayons or markers
➡ Paper taped to work surface
➡ Music (classical, rock, folk, rap, jazz, juvenile, etc.)

You and child do: Choose music to listen to while drawing. After listening to the music for a while, talk with your child about the moods and images the music evokes. Then, thinking about those moods and images, choose colors and draw scribble pictures as the music plays. Loud, full notes might evoke bright colors and heavy strokes. Gentle flute or harp music might suggest swirls of pastel colors, while drums might suggest short, zigzag lines.

■ ▲ STAINED GLASS PICTURES

You need:
- ➡ Washable black marker
- ➡ Crayons
- ➡ White paper (taped to work surface)
- ➡ Clear tape (optional)

Child does: Uses black marker to draw a simple scribble picture. (Allow marker to dry completely.) Then child fills in spaces with different bright marker or crayon colors. When using crayon, try to press fairly hard to get brightest colors. Hold Stained Glass Pictures up to light or tape pictures in a sunny window.

Variation: Child or adult can use black marker or crayon to draw traditional windows, as shown. Child then colors each square a different bright color.

■ ▲ TAKE A CLOSER LOOK—
LINES AND PICTURES

Looking at common things through a magnifying glass shows children how the ordinary can look extraordinary—a new way to look at the world.

You need:
➡ Large magnifying glass (available at drug stores)
➡ Smooth paper, construction paper, newspaper, magazines
➡ Pencil, crayons, markers, chalk, pen

Child does: Uses different writing and drawing materials to draw lines on various papers.

You and child do: Examine the lines with the magnifying glass. Your child will see that a marker line on smooth paper has fairly smooth and sharp edges, while a chalk or crayon line on construction paper looks sort of fuzzy. Talk about how different drawing materials feel, look, and behave, and how the texture and feel of the paper can affect the finished product.

Take a closer look at the print and pictures in newspapers and glossy magazines, and talk about the differences you see.

A cooperative drawing game.

You need:
→ Crayons, markers, or pencil
→ Paper

You and child do: Take turns drawing on the same piece of paper. For instance, adult draws a circle ("I'm drawing a circle.") Then child might say, "I'm drawing blue in your circle." Adult says, "I'm drawing a red, squiggly line over here." Child says, "I'm drawing dots over here." Child decides when drawing is finished.

▲ Older child variation: This game is a way to assist children who want to draw a representational picture but are not quite able to. Child may start out by drawing a circle. Adult adds eyes and nose. Child adds mouth. Adult adds simple torso. Child adds arms or legs.

● ■ ▲ WHAT TO SAY?

Even before children can draw representational art, they often have something to say about their pictures.

You need:
→ Child's artwork
→ Marker, crayon, or pencil

You and child do: Talk with your child about the artwork and let child decide if it needs a descriptive label or caption. Descriptions can be short: "Me." "Mommy and Daddy." "A bunny."

A BUNNY

2 years, 10 months

Some drawings may describe emotions: "I am happy." "I am mad." Some children will ask you to do the writing, while others will want to write on their own or with a little help. Phonetic or invented spelling is fine.

5 years

Older children may want to write a short sentence to describe the drawing more completely. Sometimes, the picture might be very simple, with a lengthy written explanation.

▲ **Older child** You or child can think up a caption *before* picture is
variation: drawn, such as "Rockets to the Moon!" or "Our family if we were all flowers."

RUBBINGS

● ■ ▲ STARTING SIMPLE

You need:
- ➡ Pencil, dark crayon, or colored chalk
- ➡ White paper
- ➡ Tape
- ➡ Flat and textured objects to rub (coins, keys, paper clips, buttons, bus tokens, paper doilies, corrugated cardboard, coarse sandpaper, rubber bands, fine string)

You do: Tape corners of paper to smooth, hard work surface.

You and child do: Slide one or two objects under paper. Show child how to lightly rub over objects with crayon, pencil, or chalk until their shape and texture appear. Very young children will need help, or may enjoy simply watching the patterns appear as you do the rubbing.

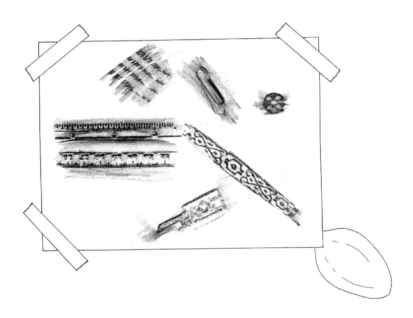

Note: Often, a rubbing works best using the side of the pencil lead or chalk, rather than the pointed end.

Also see: "Guessing Game," next.

● ■ GUESSING GAME

You need:
➡ Pencil, dark crayon, or colored chalk
➡ White paper
➡ Tape
➡ Flat and textured objects to rub (see "Starting Simple").

You do:
Tape corners of paper to smooth, hard work surface and, while child looks away, slide one or two objects under paper.

You and child do:
As you slowly rub over the object with crayon or pencil, ask your child to guess what the hidden object is. The purpose of the game is to guess the identity of the object as early as possible. If child guesses correctly, you or child can complete the rubbing. If child's guess is wrong, continue to slowly rub over the object, asking your child to look closely and take another guess.

▲ Older child variation:
Play a game of "What coin is this?" Slide a penny, nickel, dime, and quarter under the paper and ask child to try to identify coins as you rub them. You may find that coins rub best "tails" side up. Afterward, ask child to match coins to rubbings.

■ ▲ CUT-OUT RUBBING

You need:
➡ Sturdy paper cutouts, about 1 to 3 inches across (See "Fold and Cut," page 32, and "Ideas," on page 56.)
➡ White glue or glue stick
➡ Pencil, dark crayon, or chalk
➡ Two sheets of white paper (the blank sides of junk mail is fine)
➡ Tape

Note:
If using chalk, use the side of the chalk rather than the end.

You and child do:
Lightly glue paper cutouts to one sheet of paper. Cutouts can be glued down randomly, or in a particular pattern to make a design or a scene.

When glue is dry, lay second sheet of paper over cutouts and rub with crayon or pencil, until rubbings appear. (You may want to tape the second sheet of paper to the work surface.)

Ideas: Cut out small "Paper Dolls" (page 34) or "Snowflakes" (page 36), cookie cutter shapes, flowers, hearts, or free-form shapes. Use sturdy paper so you get a clear rubbing. Manila folders, index cards, or lightweight paper plates are perfect. Another source for interesting cutouts is old magazine covers. The paper cover is fairly stiff, and the pictures often feature interesting shapes.

● ■ ▲ TOUR THE HOUSE RUBBINGS

You need:
➡ Pencil or dark crayon
➡ White paper
➡ Tape (optional)

You and child do: Explore your home, looking for interesting patterns and textures to rub. Some possibilities: kitchen linoleum, bathroom tile, textured walls, bumpy countertops, bricks, or wooden floors, doors, or paneling. Smaller items to rub might include silverware patterns, a basket, strainer or colander, or a cooling rack.

Talk about how, through art, you look at and notice things you may never have noticed before.

● **Note:** When you tour the house with your tod
child to choose the objects to rub, while
actual crayon or pencil work.

● ■ ▲ NATURE/OUTDOOR RUB

You need: ➡ Pencil, dark crayon, or chalk
➡ White paper
➡ Old magazine

Note: If using chalk, use the side of the chalk ra
end.

You and
child do: Explore your yard or neighborhood, looki
ing textures for rubbings. Start off by maki
of the outside walls of your home. Then, t
walk, the driveway, bricks, flagstones, etc.

Search for natural objects to rub. A goo
might be rubbing different tree trunks to c
and smooth bark. Collect leaves, lay them
up on the magazine (this gives you a smoo
ground), cover with white paper, and rub.

TRACING

● ■ ▲ HAND OUTS

need:
- ➡ Paper
- ➡ Tape
- ➡ Pencil or crayon

**and
d do:**
Tape paper to work surface. Position child's hand on paper, fingers spread. Older children can outline their own hands, while younger children will appreciate adult help. When tracing is finished, leave plain or decorate (see "Ideas," below).

as:
- Use crayons or markers to color each finger a different color, or color the entire hand.
- Draw fingernails, and color them different colors.
- Draw rings, bracelets, or a wristwatch.
- Draw a face on each fingertip.

- Make imaginary hand animals, as shown.

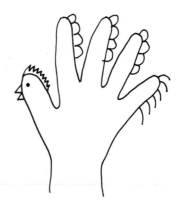

■ ▲ CUT OUT AND DRAW

You need:
→ Construction paper
→ Scissors
→ Paste, glue, or glue stick
→ Washable markers (wide tip, not fine point)

You and child do: Cut out simple shapes from one sheet of construction paper. Paper flowers, a square, circle, or triangle, or a free-form shape are all good ideas. (See "Fold and Cut," page 32). Glue paper shape to a contrasting color background, and use markers to trace around the shape, creating a clear outline. If desired, use marker to draw added details (leaves and stem for flower; facial features on a circle).

age 5

■ ▲ COOKIE CUTTER TRACERS

You need:
→ Open cookie cutters in simple shapes
→ Pencil, crayons, or washable markers
→ Paper

You and child do: A round cookie cutter is an easy shape to start with. Place it on the paper, and show child how to trace along the *inside* edge. It is helpful if an adult holds the cookie cutter steady, while the child does the tracing or coloring. (Napkins rings are a good cookie cutter substitute.)

Once child is comfortable with inside tracing, introduce tracing around the *outside* of the cookie cutter.

See also: "Fingertip Tracing" (page 80).

● ■ ▲ PEOPLE TRACING

You need:
➡ Large paper (See "Note," below.)
➡ Markers or crayons, *or*
➡ Smooth pavement and sidewalk chalk, if playing outdoors

Note: Some supermarkets will give away large sheets of butcher paper. Or, look for rolls of inexpensive white gift wrap. You can also use masking tape to tape sheets of white shelf paper together. Cut sheets of cardboard from giant-size boxes (see *"Stand It Up,"* next page). If large paper is unavailable, see "Keep It Small," next page.

You and child do: Ask child to lie down on paper or pavement. Trace around body with crayon, marker, or chalk.

Variations: *Twist and Shout.* Think about creative and funny body positions before tracing. Child can squirm around until you say "Freeze!" Or child can pretend to be running, dancing, hopping on one foot, etc.

Mirror Image. Paint or color your tracing to resemble child's features, matching eye color, hair, clothing, and accessories. If it's convenient, have child look in a mirror to describe himself/herself.

Who Am I? Decorate tracing as a clown, athlete, monster, rock star, mom, dad, or whatever child suggests.

Life-Size Paper Doll. Cut out paper clothes from construction paper or brown paper grocery bags. Clothes can match child's outfit, or can be of child's own creation. Think about hats, masks, uniforms, costumes, funny shoes, an umbrella, or other props. If available, tape gift ribbon for hair (curly or straight). You may want to cut out a life-size paper dog to keep your paper person company.

Keep It Small. Trace favorite stuffed animal or doll. Use any of above techniques to decorate.

Hang It Up. When your paper tracing is finished, you may want to cut it out and tape it to a door or wall.

Stand It Up. If you have made your tracing on stiff cardboard, attach an extra piece of cardboard to the back, to make your tracing stand up. If desired, adult can cut out tracing, using heavyweight scissors.

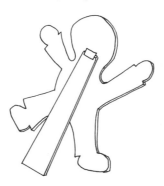

■ ▲ SHADOW TRACING

You need:
→ Bright and sunny day
→ Smooth pavement
→ Chalk

You and child do: Child stands in sunshine as you quickly outline shadow with chalk. Child might enjoy holding some sort of prop, such as a tennis racquet, a helium balloon on a string, or an umbrella. Try tracing the shadows of two children holding hands.

A daytime activity.

You need:
→ A window (sunny or cloudy)
→ A simple line drawing
→ Tape
→ Lightweight white paper
→ Pencil, markers, or crayons

Child does: Chooses or creates a line drawing or picture to copy.

You do: Tape the line drawing to a sunny window. Tape a piece of white paper over the drawing at the top corners, leaving the bottom loose.

! Caution: Remind child not to lean on or push hard on the window.

Child does: Traces drawing with pencil, crayon, or marker. Lift white paper to check if entire picture has been traced. Then remove white paper and color in picture.

FUN WITH CHALK

● ■ ▲ GETTING TO KNOW YOU

Chalk is fun because it's so different from familiar crayons, pencils, and markers. Chalk feels, looks, and sounds different. It smudges and breaks easily. Supply smocks, roll up sleeves, and be sure your child understands that it's okay when chalk breaks.

You need:
→ Chalk (Colored chalk is nice, but not necessary.)
→ White paper
→ Construction paper
→ Brown paper grocery bags (optional)
→ Corrugated cardboard (optional)

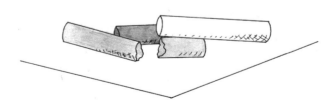

You and child do: Experiment with different ways of using dry chalk:
- Draw on smooth white paper, construction paper, brown paper bags, or pieces cut from cardboard boxes.
- Draw with the end of the chalk. Then draw with the side of the chalk.
- When chalk breaks, use fingers to rub the crumbs and powder into your paper, to make smudges.
- If working with colored chalk, mix colors by drawing and rubbing with fingers.
- Draw thin lines and smudge them by rubbing with fingers, cotton swab, cotton ball, or paper towel.

How to erase chalk: When drawing with *dry* chalk on *smooth white paper,* you can erase by wiping lightly with a damp paper towel.

■ ▲ WET AND DRY

Your child will discover that drawing with wet chalk feels different and produces different results.

You need:
- ➡ Chalk (colored is best)
- ➡ White, smooth paper
- ➡ Construction paper (black or dark colors)
- ➡ Water
- ➡ Small bowl
- ➡ Hair dryer (optional)

You and child do: Dip chalk in water and draw on dry paper. Then, draw with dry chalk on a piece of wet or damp paper. Child can decide which technique is the most fun, and which makes the brightest drawings. Allow drawings to dry. (If desired, you can speed drying with a hair dryer.)

■ ▲ SUGAR-WATER DRAWINGS

You need:
- ➡ Colored chalk
- ➡ Smooth, white paper or construction paper
- ➡ Sugar-water solution ($1/4$ cup sugar dissolved in $1/2$ cup water)

! You do: Drop a few pieces of chalk in the sugar-water solution and microwave for 30 seconds on High. Let cool for a few minutes and remove chalk.

Child does: Draws with soaked chalk pieces, occasionally dipping chalk in cooled sugar-water solution. Chalk will appear brighter and won't smudge as much.

Liquid starch variation: Dip or soak chalk in liquid starch before drawing, for a similar effect.

● ■ ▲ CHALK AND WATER PRINTS

You need:
➡ Dark construction paper (Smooth, white paper won't work!)
➡ Chalk (white or pastel)
➡ Water
➡ Things to print with (sponge, leaves, hand print, cotton swabs)

You and child do: Rub hard with side of chalk to cover the center section of paper, leaving a border around edges.

Print with damp sponge, hand, foot, leaf, or any other damp object that will pick up the chalk dust. *Print will fade or disappear as paper dries.* Chalky paper may be printed on again.

Variations:
- Dip cotton swabs in water and "paint" on chalky paper. Again, design will fade as paper dries.

- Print or paint with the sugar-water solution from "Sugar-Water Drawings" (page 63) for longer-lasting results.

See also: "Water Prints" (page 98).

■ ▲ CHALK AND GLUE PRINTS

This technique will create a more permanent and shiny print than "Chalk and Water Prints," *(preceding section).*

You need:
- ➡ Dark construction paper (Smooth, white paper won't work!)
- ➡ Chalk (white or pastel)
- ➡ White glue
- ➡ Small paintbrush or cotton swabs
- ➡ Things to print with (sponge, leaves, hand print)

You and child do:
To create a permanent print, follow directions for "Chalk and Water Prints" (preceding section), covering paper with chalk. Use paintbrush or cotton swab to paint a thin coat of glue on surface of object you plan to print. Place object, glue side down, onto chalky surface. Press with fingers and lift to reveal print. Allow glue to dry.

FUN WITH DRAWING

● ■ ▲ MEMORY GAMES

● ■ *Colors.* Sit across from your child, with crayons or markers between you. Each player has a supply of scrap paper, cut into 3-inch squares. Choose a crayon or marker, draw a dot, line, or scribble on a paper square, and show it to your child. Then hide your drawing and ask your child to make a scribble or mark of the same color. Repeat with different colors.

Make the game more difficult by drawing with two, three, or four colors on the same paper square. Your child must remember all the colors and draw them on his or her own paper square.

■ ▲ *Lines and Shapes.* Sit across from your child with crayons or markers between you. Each player has a supply of scrap paper, cut into 3-inch squares. Draw a line (straight, wiggly, zigzag) or a simple shape (square, triangle, circle) and show the drawing to your child. Then hide your drawing and ask your child to draw the same shape. Make the game more difficult by asking your child to duplicate both the shape *and* the color that you used. Or draw more complicated designs (a circle inside square; a square with a line through it). Finally, switch roles and ask your child to draw shapes while *you* remember and duplicate them.

▲ *Objects.* Choose a very simple household object (ball, spoon, cup, crayon) and let your child take a close look at it. Then hide the object and ask your child to try to draw the object from memory. When the drawing is finished, it's your child's turn to choose an object, and your turn to draw.

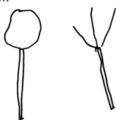

"A spoon and a fork"

▲ DRAWING YOUR ABCs

A fun and easy game that you can play anywhere!

You need:
➡ Paper (Junk mail is fine.)
➡ Markers, crayons, or pencil

Child does: Picks a number between 1 and 26.

You and child do: Figure out which letter of the alphabet corresponds to the number your child chose. For instance, 4 is the letter *D*, 7 is the letter *G*, and so on. Then, ask your child to think up and draw two or three things that start with that letter. When drawing is finished, child chooses another number.

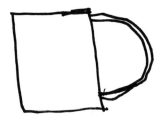 

"Mommy's cup and our calico cat"

■ ▲ TINY PICTURES

You need:
➡ Small pieces of paper, 4 × 4 inches or smaller
➡ Pencil, pen, markers, or crayons
➡ Construction paper and glue or tape (optional)

Child does: Children will enjoy the idea of making "Tiny Pictures" for a change of pace. Young artists often like to use pencil or pen because of the fine tip, inspired by the small space to fill. Tiny Pictures often end up having a surprising amount of detail. Mount two to four Tiny Pictures together on a sheet of colorful construction paper. (See next page.)

● ■ ▲ GIANT PICTURE

You need:
➡ Large paper, about 2 × 3 feet (See "Note" in "People Tracing," page 60).
➡ Masking tape
➡ Washable markers or crayons

You do: A sliding glass door is a great spot for this activity, or lay paper on a smooth floor. If paper is taped vertically to a door, give child a footstool. If paper is taped horizontally, it's perfect for two or three kids to draw at the same time.

Child does: This is a chance for kids to draw long lines and TALL drawings, almost as big as themselves.

● ■ ▲ FOIL PICTURE

You need: ➡ Aluminum foil
➡ Scissors
➡ White or construction paper
➡ Tape (clear or masking)
➡ Washable markers
➡ Paper towels

You do: Cut foil into a square, approximately 5 × 5 inches. Tape foil, shiny side up, to center of paper, being sure to tape all edges.

Child does: Uses washable markers to draw on foil. Colors will have a shiny, metallic look.

You do: To reuse foil or to erase part of the drawing, rub with dry paper towel.

Child does: If desired, child can decorate paper border, which serves as a frame for the picture.

Note: These drawings take a long time to dry, but may be hung up on display while wet.

See also: "Foil Print" (page 112).

▲ PEEKABOO PICTURE

You need: ➡ Two pieces of paper (same size)
➡ Markers, crayons, or pencil
➡ Tape (clear or masking)
➡ Scissors (optional)

Child does: Draws a picture on one piece of paper, thinking about where peekaboo doors might go. (See "Ideas," next page.)

You and child do: Cut or tear three-sided "doors," as shown. Place drawing over second piece of paper, and tape edges.

Child does: Draws tiny pictures or writes messages inside peekaboo doors.

"A robot with dials inside, holding a ray gun and chocolate milk"—Dave, age 5

Ideas:
- Draw a house and cut peekaboo doors at the door and windows. Draw tiny people inside.
- Draw a big tree and cut a few peekaboo doors in the trunk or leaves. Draw animals inside.
- Draw a robot and cut a peekaboo window in its chest. Draw circuitry, buttons, and dials inside.
- Draw a mountainside and cut a peekaboo door for a secret cave. Draw whatever or whoever lives in the secret cave.
- Draw a treasure box and cut a peekaboo door for the lid. Draw jewels and coins inside.
- Draw a self-portrait and cut a peekaboo door in the tummy. Draw your favorite foods inside.

■ ▲ FOLD-UP PICTURE

You need:
- ➡ Stiff paper (Old manila folders work well.)
- ➡ Crayons or markers
- ➡ Sharp scissors

Child does: On stiff paper, child draws a simple drawing that features one or two objects. A house, a car, a person, or a tree are good ideas, although scribble drawings work well too. Older children may want to color in the background, adding sky, grass, sunshine, etc.

You do: Cut out the main figure or object in the picture, leaving the bottom of the figure *uncut*.

Child does: Bends cut-out section up for a three-dimensional effect.

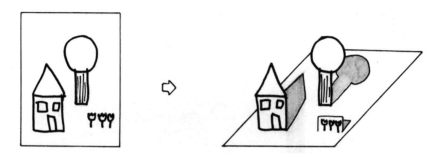

▲ ANIMAL ALPHABET

You need: ➡ Paper
➡ Markers, crayons, pencil, or pen

You and child do: Write child's name in capital letters. Add simple details to turn each letter into an animal, real or imaginary.

For more of a challenge, write a letter, think up an animal that begins with that letter, and then try to turn the letter into that animal.

Shark

Butterfly

▲ MAKE A SCENE

You need:
➡ Paper
➡ Markers or crayons
➡ Old magazines with colorful pictures
➡ Scissors
➡ Glue, paste, or glue stick

Child does: Draws simple background scene (mountains, house, city streets, ocean or lake, etc.). Try not to include any details. A picture of sky, grass, and the sun is fine.

You and child do: Cut out magazine pictures (cars, people, animals, etc.) and glue or paste them to background picture to make a scene, either real-looking or imaginary.

▲ 3-D PICTURE

You need:
- ➡ Paper
- ➡ Washable markers
- ➡ White glue and clear tape
- ➡ Household items for picture (cotton balls, toothpicks, cotton swabs, plastic bottle caps, pipe cleaners, drinking straws, yarn, gift ribbon, string, Popsicle sticks, etc.)

Child does: Draws a simple background, as in "Make a Scene" (preceding section).

You and child do: Glue or tape household items to drawing, creating a three-dimensional scene. See "Ideas," next page. Child can then draw added features or details.

73

Ideas:
- Fill a blue sky with cotton-ball clouds and a bottle-cap sun.
- Use cotton balls to make snow or a snowman.
- Tape drinking straws to paper for telephone poles or flower stems.
- Glue down a cut-out paper kite, flying from yarn or string.
- Make a fence with toothpicks or cotton swabs broken in half.
- Tape down sections of mesh onion bags for window screens, tennis nets, or spider webs.

▲ IMPOSSIBLE PICTURES

You need:
- ➡ Paper
- ➡ Markers, crayons, pencil, or pen

Child does: Thinks up and draws an impossible and funny situation. Some suggestions are:

- A dog driving a car
- An upside-down house
- Mom and Dad are little and the kids are big
- Riding bicycles on the ocean

● ■ ▲ MAKE A SCRAPBOOK

A bound book of artwork is fun to make and even more fun to show to appreciative audiences. Or, your child may choose to give it as a gift.

You need:
- ➡ Construction paper
- ➡ Stapler
- ➡ Masking tape, colored fabric tape, or colored plastic tape
- ➡ Plain paper *or* drawings, each measuring 5 × 8 inches or smaller
- ➡ Markers or crayons
- ➡ Clear tape

Child does: Chooses three or four favorite colors of construction paper.
You do: Stack construction paper and fold all sheets in half. Staple along folded edge, as shown. Cover both sides of stapled edge with heavy tape. Write scrapbook title and child's name on cover.

Ideas:

● *First Art Book.* Choose from existing collection of drawings and paintings (scribble pictures are fine), or your child can create new drawings to tape into the book.

■ ▲ *My Family.* Child draws pictures of family members, pets, home, and relatives on 5 × 7-inch sheets of paper. Tape each drawing to a separate page. Older child or adult can label each drawing with appropriate name.

■ ▲ *A Day in the Life of Me.* Child draws pictures of favorite activities, friends, places, foods, etc. on 5 × 7-inch sheets of paper. Tape pictures into book and label with a word or two, or a short sentence.

▲ *On the Road (Travel Journal).* This is a good activity for a long car ride. Child draws small pictures of sights from car window, to be mounted in book and labeled, if desired.

6
PAINTING

● ■ ▲ FINGERPAINT RECIPE, TECHNIQUES, AND TIPS

Flour Paste Fingerpaint. This is an easy and economical way to stretch the fingerpaint you have or create a thick fingerpaint from more watery poster paints. In a small bowl, combine ¼ cup of flour with ¼ cup of water to make a thick, syrupy, smooth paste. Add 2 to 3 teaspoons of paint for color, and spoon paint onto paper.

Techniques and Tips. Fingerpainting is best done standing up. Children should wear long smocks, with sleeves pushed above elbows, but the best advice is to wear old clothes that can get painty! Have soapy water and paper towels handy for cleanup.

Glossy or plastic-backed paper is best. Good sources are butcher paper, shelf paper, or inexpensive rolls of white gift wrap, but any sturdy, *smooth* paper will work. Try to find large sheets of paper.

Paper Plate Paintings. If paper isn't available, white paper plates are a fast, easy, and fun background for making lots of miniature fingerpaintings. Mess is minimal, and the paintings are easy to move around, take home, or hang up!

Preparation. Use a clean sponge to wet paper before painting. You may want to dampen your work surface first, to keep the paper (or paper plate) from slipping. Be careful not to use too much paint at one time, or painting will be too thick and gloppy to show finger marks and will take too long to dry.

● ■ STARTING OFF

You need:
→ Fingerpaint (one or two colors)
→ Paper (white, smooth finish)

You and child do: Allow children to fingerpaint in their own style, at their own pace. Some kids will dive into it with enthusiasm and gusto, while others are less comfortable with the mess. Painting *with* your child may help a reluctant artist. You can do the initial "smearing" and let your child draw designs with one or two fingers. Eventually, your child will decide that smearing is fun too.

See also: "Shaving Cream Painting" (page 82) might appeal more to children reluctant to get messy.

● ■ PATTERN MAKERS

You need:
➡ Styrofoam grocery trays *or* heavyweight paper plates
➡ Scissors
➡ Wet fingerpainting

You and child do: Cut Styrofoam tray or paper plate into sizes easily held by child. (A 2 × 2-inch piece works well.) Cut tabs, fringe, points, etc. along one edge, as shown. Styrofoam tabs will snap off easily.

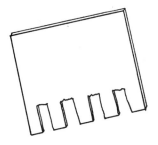

Drag the cut edge through the fingerpainting to create different patterns. Show child how to make straight stripes, wavy stripes, criss-cross stripes, and so on.

Variation: Press cookie cutters onto fingerpainting, moving them slightly from side to side, to make patterns.

● ■ ▲ FINGERTIP TRACING

You need:
- ➡ Fingerpaint
- ➡ Paper (white, smooth finish)
- ➡ Plastic cups and containers (round and square)
- ➡ Open cookie cutters (optional)
- ➡ Cotton swabs (optional)

You and child do: Cover paper with fingerpaint. Turn cup or container upside down onto painting and hold it steady with one hand, as you show your child how to trace around the edge with a fingertip.

Variations: • Lay your hand on the painting. Use your other hand to help child trace around your fingers. Then help child to trace his or her own hand.

• If available, press simple cookie cutter shapes into the painting, and show child how to make a fingertip tracing outside the cookie cutter.
• *Cotton swab tracing*—Use a cotton swab to trace a hand print, or to trace the outside or inside of open cookie cutters.

● ■ ▲ CRAYON COVER

You need: ➡ Crayon drawing (on smooth-finish, white paper)
➡ Fingerpaint
➡ Paper towel (optional)

Note: This works best with a crayon drawing that was made by pressing fairly hard with the crayons.

Child does: Covers crayon drawing with fingerpaint. Rubs with fingers to see crayon drawing show through the paint.

Note: If crayon drawing doesn't readily show through, use either a dry hand or a dry paper towel to wipe away excess paint.

Ideas: • This is a fast and fun way to make "Scribble Drawings" (page 48) more colorful and festive!

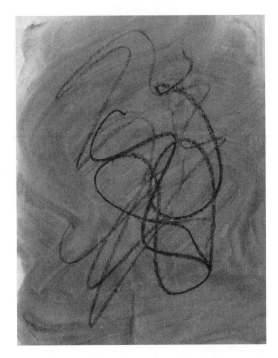

- Use crayons to draw an underwater scene (fish, people swimming, mermaids) and cover the drawing with blue fingerpaint.
- This is an easy way to fill in the sky or grass. Make a crayon drawing of a rainbow and cover with blue paint. Or draw a crayon drawing of a house and cover with green paint on the bottom and blue paint on the top.

See also: "Crayon Resist" (page 88).

■ ▲ SHAVING CREAM PAINTING

You need: ➡ Shaving cream
➡ Cookie sheet

You and child do: Squirt a medium amount of shaving cream on cookie sheet and let child smear it around like fingerpaint. Add more shaving cream as needed. Unlike paint, shaving cream holds its shape and children can create texture as well as patterns. When painting is done, warm water washes hands and cookie sheet clean.

● ■ ▲ PAINTS, BRUSHES, AND SETTING UP

Paints. Washable, nontoxic children's liquid paints are available in supermarkets and drug stores and are wonderfully versatile. Straight from the container, you can use the paint as fingerpaint or thick poster paint. It can also be watered down, and colors mix easily. Other paints to look for are traditional poster paints and watercolor kits.

Brushes. Think about visiting an art supply or craft store for a couple of good-quality brushes. Inexpensive brushes sold with watercolor kits often make painting difficult because the brush doesn't hold much water or paint.

Paper. Choose paper with a smooth finish. While newsprint is fine for beginner projects, paint adheres better and colors look nicer on better-quality white paper. The back of junk mail is a good source, or buy paper in supermarkets, drug stores, or toy stores.

When fingerpainting, glossy or plastic coated paper is best. (Look for butcher paper, shelf paper, or rolls of inexpensive white gift wrap.) If glossy paper is hard to find, use any white paper with a smooth finish that won't readily absorb water.

Setting Up. Pour one or more small puddles of liquid paint on a dish. This prevents spills, minimizes mess, and saves paint. It also keeps kids from dipping a red painty brush into a jar of yellow paint!

Provide a wide-mouthed jar of water for rinsing brushes, and a pad of paper towels for blotting the brush after rinsing it.

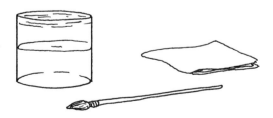

● LINES AND BLOBS

You need:
- Liquid paint
- Saucer
- Paintbrush
- Paper
- Tape

You do: Tape paper to work surface. Pour a small puddle of paint onto a saucer.

You and child do: Show child how to dip brush in paint and apply it to paper. Children can experiment with different brush techniques: dragging, pushing, slapping, dabbing, rolling, etc.

You need only provide one paint color for first-time painters. They will have plenty of fun and challenge, simply dipping the brush and spreading color on paper. When older children are ready for more colors, pour two or three small puddles of paint on a dinner plate, and let kids dip, mix, and choose colors as they please. Some kids will enjoy painting the plate!

Dave's first painting—age 2

● ■ ▲ WET PAPER PAINTING

You need:
- Paper
- Wet sponge
- Liquid paint
- Paintbrush

You and child do:	You may want to dampen work surface first, to keep paper from slipping around. Then dampen paper thoroughly with wet sponge.
Child does:	Paints on the wet paper. Encourage your child to experiment with different colors to see how they blend together. Talk about how painting on wet paper is different from painting on dry paper.

● ■ ▲ BUMPY PAINT

Use salt and your microwave to produce surprising results!

You need:
- ➡ Children's liquid paint or poster paint
- ➡ Salt
- ➡ Measuring spoons
- ➡ Small dishes
- ➡ Paintbrush
- ➡ Smooth-finish white paper *or* white paper plate
- ➡ Microwave oven

You and child do:	Pour 1 tablespoon of paint on dish. Add 1 teaspoon of salt to paint, and mix with brush. Mixture should be fairly thick.
Child does:	Paints a free-form painting using paint-salt mixture. Encourage your child to paint some parts of the picture using *lots* of paint, applying paint thickly.
! You do:	When painting is done, place it in the microwave and bake on High for 10 to 30 seconds, watching carefully. Paint will bubble up and dry with an interesting and bumpy texture.

■ ▲ CRACKLE PAINT

You need:
- ➡ Children's liquid paint or poster paint (Only one color is fine.)
- ➡ Salt
- ➡ Small dish
- ➡ Measuring spoons
- ➡ Paintbrush
- ➡ White paper plate, Styrofoam grocery tray, or smooth-finish white paper
- ➡ Crayons
- ➡ Microwave oven

You and child do: Pour 1 tablespoon of paint into dish, and use your paintbrush to mix in 1 teaspoon of salt. Mixture will be fairly thick.

Choose crayons that are contrasting colors from your paint. Pressing hard, cover the plate, tray, or paper with stripes, swirls, or blocks of bright color. It is important to have a heavy coating of crayon.

Then paint over your crayon coloring with the paint-salt mixture. Dab the paint on in a splotchy manner, rather than painting with smooth strokes.

! You do: Place painted plate or tray in microwave and bake on High for 10 to 15 seconds, watching carefully. Paint will "crackle up," become textured, and reveal splotches of crayon color.

■ ▲ SCRATCH PAINTING

You need:
→ Cardboard milk or juice containers (Any size, but half gallon provides a larger painting surface.)
→ Scissors
→ Paper towels
→ Dinner plate
→ Children's liquid paint or poster paint (1–3 dark colors)
→ Liquid dish detergent
→ Crayons (optional)
→ Paintbrush
→ Microwave oven (optional)
→ Paper plate (optional)

You do: Wash and rinse cardboard container, and cut out one or two sides, as shown. Dry inside surface of cut-out section with paper towel.

Pour about a teaspoon of each color paint on the dinner plate. Mix one drop of liquid detergent into each teaspoon of paint.

Child does: If desired, child can use crayons to color blank side of cardboard piece. A scribble picture is fine, or just fill the area with blocks of bright color.

Then cover the crayon drawing (or plain blank cardboard) with the paint-detergent mixture, painting freely and mixing colors for a colorful and fun effect.

! • You do: Allow paint to dry completely. If you're in a hurry, you can bake your painted cardboard in the microwave on High, for about 30 seconds.

When paint is dry, use a toothpick, tip of paintbrush handle, or similar utensil to scratch designs through paint, so milk carton surface (or crayon coloring) shows through. The following example was made from a two-side section of a milk carton.

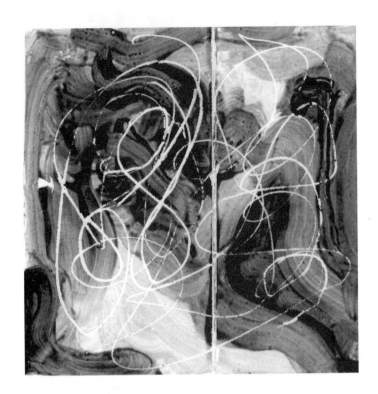

Paper plate variation: If a juice or milk carton isn't available, a paper plate works well, too. However, you *must* color the plate with crayon colors before painting.

■ ▲ CRAYON RESIST

You need:
→ Smooth-finish, white paper
→ Crayons
→ Liquid paint, poster paint, or water colors
→ Paintbrush

You do: Thin liquid or poster paints with a little water.

Child does: Draws a crayon scribble picture, pressing fairly hard with the crayons.

Paints over crayon picture with one or more colors, watching as crayon drawing comes through.

Variations: *Magic Painting.* Use white crayon to draw a simple picture or message on white paper. Drawing will appear invisible until colorful paint is applied.

Markers and Crayons. Follow the preceding directions but use washable markers instead of paints. This works especially well for a fast and easy "Magic Painting."

▲ COLOR IT IN

You need:
- Smooth-finish, white paper
- Tape
- Black or dark crayon or marker
- Liquid paint or water colors
- Paintbrush

You do: Tape paper to work surface.

Child does: Draws scribble picture with crayon or marker. Fills in spaces with brightly colored paints, as in "Stained Glass Pictures" (page 50).

Note: It doesn't matter at all when your child paints "over the lines" of the crayon or marker drawing. Crayon will resist the paint, marker will blend with the paint, and the colors will combine for an interesting effect.

■ ▲ PAINTING ON FOIL

You need:
- Children's liquid or poster paint
- Liquid dish detergent
- Dinner plate
- Paintbrush
- Water
- Aluminum foil
- Masking tape

You do: For each color, mix about 1 teaspoon of paint with one or two drops of detergent, directly on the dinner plate. Three colors are plenty. Tape edges of foil to work surface.

Child does: Paints on foil. Allow to air dry.

Ideas: • Before painting, cover a piece of cardboard with foil, to provide a stiff and more permanent painting surface.
                 • Before painting, gently crumple foil and then smooth it out again. Added texture creates an interesting effect.

• When painting is finished, carefully peel tape up and fold over to create a simple and instant picture frame.
• If paint doesn't adhere well to foil, add one more drop of dish detergent.

See also: "Foil Print" (page 112).

You need: → Heavyweight paper (paper plates, manila folders, magazine covers)
→ Paper (white or construction)
→ Scissors
→ Liquid paint and paintbrush
→ Sponge piece (Cut a 1-inch wide section from end of sponge.)

You and child do: Follow "Fold and Cut" instructions (page 32) to cut shapes in heavyweight paper. Brush a small amount of paint onto end of sponge piece. Place stencil over paper to be painted. Adult can hold stencil still, as child gently dabs painty sponge up and down, over stencil. Lift stencil to reveal print.

Note: Children will need a few practice prints to figure out how much paint is needed, and the best way to use the sponge. Experiment with different sponge techniques such as pressing hard or pressing gently, dabbing, dragging, or swirling the sponge on the paper.

Variation: After you've made a few stencil prints, the stencil itself will be pretty painty. Turn it over and press the painty stencil on paper. Lift to reveal a "negative" print!

▲ BLEACH PAINTING

! Caution: *This activity uses bleach. Close adult supervision is necessary at all times. Protect clothing and work surface in case of spills.*

You need:
→ Household bleach
→ Small bowl
→ Dark construction paper (black, blue, brown, green)
→ Tape
→ Cotton swabs

You do: Pour about 1 tablespoon of bleach into bowl. Tape construction paper to work surface. Remind child to be careful when using bleach.

You and child do: Dip one end of cotton swab in bleach and paint designs on construction paper. Paper will lighten as you paint.

● ■ ▲ WHO NEEDS BRUSHES?

Art is fun and can be funny. Think up creative ways to paint without using a traditional paintbrush.

You need:
→ Paintbrush substitutes (cotton swabs, sponge pieces, fingers, leaves, twigs, scraps of fabric, paper, cardboard, and so on)

➚ Smooth-finish paper

➚ Children's liquid paint

Child does: Uses paintbrush substitutes to make a free-form picture, noticing the different patterns, designs, and textures created with the different "brushes."

Fingerpaint variation: Cover the paper with a layer of fingerpaint. Drag, press, or roll different objects (comb, cardboard, pine cone, golf ball, tennis ball) along the surface of the painty paper, to create patterns and texture.

See also: "Pattern Makers" (page 79), "Drip and Tip Painting," (below), "Blow Painting" (page 94), and "Marble Painting" (page 95).

● ■ ▲ DRIP AND TIP PAINTING

You need: ➚ Children's liquid paint, thinned with water so that it's very thin and runny
➚ Paper (smooth finish, rather than absorbent)
➚ Cookie sheet or shoe box lid
➚ Tape (clear or masking)
➚ Teaspoon or paintbrush

You and child do: Tape paper to cookie sheet, as shown. Use a teaspoon or paintbrush to dribble and drip runny paint all over the paper. Then help child to tip cookie sheet side to side, and front to back, so paint runs over the paper.

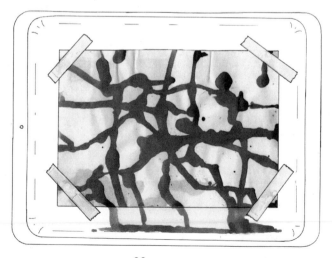

Pour off any excess paint, and repeat process with a contrasting color, painting over first color.

Replace paper and repeat process, this time using two or three colors at the same time.

▲ BLOW PAINTING

You need:
➡ Children's liquid paint or poster paint, thinned with water so that it's fairly runny
➡ Paper (smooth finish, rather than absorbent)
➡ Cookie sheet or shoe box lid
➡ Tape (clear or masking)
➡ Paintbrush
➡ Drinking straw
➡ Teaspoon

You and child do:
Tape paper to cookie sheet or box lid. Use the paintbrush to drip paint all over the paper, as shown (1). As adult holds drinking straw close to paint puddles, child blows into straw, causing paint to spread over the paper (2).

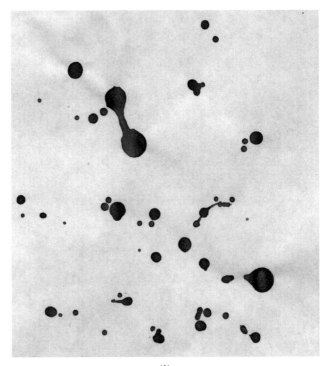

(1)

(2)

If desired, repeat process with a contrasting color, painting over first color.

Variations:
- Repeat preceding technique, starting with two or three colors at the same time.
- Position the straw *above* the paint puddles, so child can blow directly down onto paint. Then position straw at an angle, so child sees the different results.

! Note: Older children can hold the straw themselves. Younger children should have adult help holding the straw, to prevent possibility of children accidentally sucking up paint!

■ ▲ MARBLE PAINTING

This is fun to do and exciting to watch!

You need:
➡ White paper
➡ Shoe box lid, cookie sheet, or cake or pie pan
➡ Small bowls or saucers
➡ Liquid paint
➡ Marbles
➡ Teaspoon (optional)

You and child do: Line the bottom of the shoe box lid, cookie sheet, or pan with white paper. The paper should fit the pan.

Pour a small amount of liquid paint into several bowls, a different color in each bowl. Primary colors (blue, yellow, and red) work well.

Drop one marble into each bowl and coat the marbles with color. Use fingers or teaspoon to drop painty marbles onto the white paper (one at a time or all at once), and roll them around until they no longer print or your child feels that the painting is finished. In the examples below, the painting on the left was made with three marbles, while the painting on the right was made with six marbles.

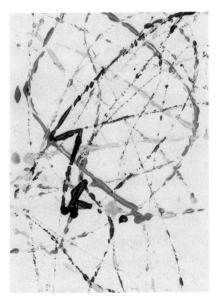

Variation: Try using two marbles for each color, or one marble for one color and two marbles for another color.

7
PRINTING

● ■ ▲ MAKE A PRINTING PAD

Fold a paper towel in quarters, wet it, and squeeze the water out. Open the wet towel to quarter size again and flatten it onto a plate, tray, or aluminum foil (to protect your work surface). Pour a small amount of liquid paint onto the paper towel and spread with a paintbrush or fingers.

You'll get a better print if you slide a few layers of newspaper under the paper to receive the print.

Remind children not to press objects too deeply into the printing pad. Too much paint makes for a smudged print.

Remind children that printing results in a *backward* or reversed image.

● ■ WATER PRINTS

The easiest printing of all.

You need:
➡ Dark construction paper
➡ Bowl of water
➡ Things to print (sponge, paper towel, fabric scraps, cup, blocks, etc.)

You and child do: Dip objects in water, squeeze gently, and then press onto dark construction paper to create a water print. Print wet hands or feet. Make wet sponge prints. Fold a paper towel into a sturdy roll, wet it, and print. Dip the rim of a cup in water and print circles. Dip wooden blocks in water and print shapes. Dip yarn in water, squeeze, and then press onto paper. Then watch as prints dry and disappear.

See also: "Chalk and Water Prints" (page 64).

Variations: *Outdoor Water Prints.* A summer's day around the wading pool, or a walk after a rainstorm is an opportunity for outdoor printing. Wet hand prints and footprints on warm (not hot!) pavement are fun to make and fun to watch as they disappear in the sun. After a rainstorm, when pavement has just dried, search for wet leaves still plastered to the pavement. Lift these leaves to see the wet prints beneath. Find a puddle to walk through and then leave a trail of boot prints.

This is a good way to get used to printing with a printing pad filled with paint.

You need: ➡ Printing pad with paint (See "Make a Printing Pad")
➡ Paper

Child does: Presses fingers, thumbs, or entire hand onto printing pad and then prints on paper. Child can experiment with hand pressure and amount of paint, to see which technique produces the best-looking prints.

Ideas:
- If printing on paper with a smooth finish, see if child can produce fingerprints. (This requires a light touch on the printing pad and a medium touch on the paper.) Use a magnifying glass to see prints more clearly.
- Add marker or crayon detail to create "Thumbprint Bumblebees" or "Fingerprint Flowers."

- Make "Tiny Elf Feet" by printing side of child's fist (1). Then print child's thumbprint for big toe (2). Finally, add three or four fingertip prints for the other toes (3).

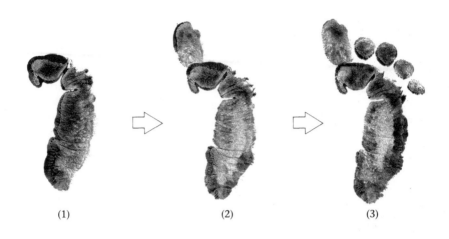

(1)   (2)   (3)

● ■ ▲ KITCHEN PRINTS

You need: ➡ Printing pad with paint (See "Make a Printing Pad," page 98.)
➡ Paper
➡ Kitchen supplies to print with (See "Ideas," below.)

Child does: Gathers selection of kitchen utensils, throwaways, and food items to print with.

Ideas: *Flatware.* Press the back of a fork onto the printing pad and print. If the handles of your flatware have an obvious pattern, see if it will print. The items pictured below are the handle of a butter knife, a fork, and a cake server.

Circles and squares. Collect round and square kitchen items to print. Use rims of cups, cans, bottles, plastic milk bottle caps, or the end of the cardboard tube from paper towels. For squares or rectangles, try printing different edges of a sponge, rectangular spice cans, or the small ends of empty food boxes.

Creative kitchenware. Look around your kitchen for unusual items to print. Try printing a plastic dish scrubber or the bristles of a small scrub brush. Print a plastic or metal spatula, a tea strainer, or roll a small whisk on the printing pad and then on paper.

Cookie shapes. Press cookie cutters into a printing pad loaded with fairly thick liquid paint. Print as before.

Fruits and veggies. Cut vegetables and fruits in half, and press the cut sides into printing pad. Try cross sections of onions, apples, limes, lemons, peppers, zucchini, and more.

Toys. Plastic toys can be easily washed. Print magnetic plastic letters, different sizes and shapes of plastic blocks, plastic rings, etc.

● ■ ▲ FOLDOVER PRINTS

You need:
➡ Paper (plain or construction)
➡ Liquid paint and paintbrush
➡ Rolling pin, smooth-sided drinking glass, or cardboard tube from paper towels (optional)

You and child do: Fold paper in half, crease, and open up.

Child does: Paints a simple design or picture on *one* side of the paper only, using one to three colors. (Try not to let paint dry!)

You and child do: Fold unpainted paper over painting and roll gently with rolling pin or glass. (You can also press with your hands.) Open paper up to see print.

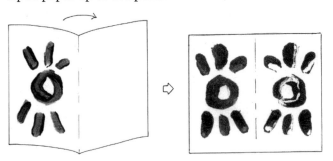

Notes: If your print isn't dark enough, fold paper over and press again.

Talk about the different results you get when you use lots of paint versus little paint, or roll over the paper pressing heavily versus gently.

● ■ ▲ BLOT PRINTS

You need:
→ Two pieces of paper (plain or construction)
→ Liquid paint and paintbrush
→ Rolling pin, smooth-sided drinking glass, or cardboard tube from paper towels (optional)

Child does: Paints a simple design or picture on paper, using brush or fingers.

You and child do: Lay second piece of paper over painting, and roll gently with rolling pin, glass, or tube. (Or press with hand.) Peel second sheet to see print. If desired, child can add more details or colors to first painting and make another print.

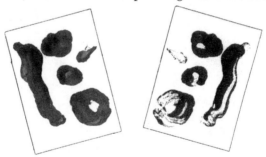

▲ STRING FOLDOVERS

You need:
→ Paper (plain or construction)
→ Yarn
→ Liquid paint
→ Small bowls
→ Paintbrush (optional)
→ Rolling pin, smooth-sided drinking glass, or cardboard tube from paper towels

You and child do: Fold the paper in half, crease, and open up. Pour a small amount of liquid paint into a bowl, and add a little water to thin the paint. Cut a 2- to 3-foot length of yarn and dip it into the paint. Use a paintbrush or your fingers to stir the yarn into the paint so it absorbs the color. Holding the yarn over the bowl, run the yarn gently through your fingers, squeezing out most of the watery paint.

Hold one end of the paint-covered yarn and lower it onto one side of the paper. Fold the paper over the yarn and roll gently with the rolling pin, glass, or cardboard tube. Open up and remove yarn to see your print.

If desired, soak a second length of yarn in a different color paint and repeat process.

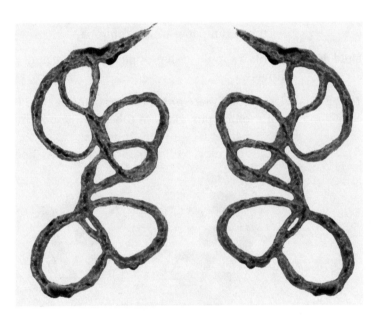

Variation: Dip two or three lengths of yarn in separate colors and place on paper together. Fold paper over and roll as before.

■ ▲ SOAP PRINTS

You need:
➡ Printing pad with fairly thick paint (See "Make a Printing Pad," page 98.)
➡ Paper
➡ Paper towels
➡ Fresh bar of soap
➡ Dull pencil
➡ Butter knife

Note: It is important to use a very *fresh,* new bar of soap. If the soap isn't fresh, it will splinter when you try to carve it.

You and child do: Use the dull pencil point to carve simple designs (lines, dots, etc.) in one end of the bar of soap.

Layer two or three paper towels on your work surface, and lay the paper to be printed on top of them. Press the carved soap edge into the printing pad and print on paper.

When child tires of that design, cut off that carved edge and carve again, or carve a new design on a different edge. To print with a new color, rinse painty bar of soap with cold water and dry with a paper towel.

Note: You may want to wrap part of the bar of soap in a dry paper towel for a better grip.

▲ SANDPAPER CRAYON PRINT

These prints are especially pretty when hung in a sunny window!

You need:
- ➡ Sandpaper (100- to 150-grit)
- ➡ Scissors
- ➡ Crayons
- ➡ White paper
- ➡ Newspaper
- ➡ Iron

You do: Cut out a small to medium piece of sandpaper, no larger than a 5-inch square.

Child does: Draws colorful picture, designs, or scribbles on sandpaper, pressing hard with crayon. (Adult may want to go over drawing with more crayon, to ensure a good print.)

Place sandpaper, drawing side up, on several thicknesses of newspaper.

You do: Cover with white paper, and press with a warm iron for about 10 to 15 seconds, until color comes through the paper.

A second print can be made, but it will be lighter. For darker reprints, use crayons to color the sandpaper drawing again.

Variations: Experiment with printing on different kinds of paper: paper towels, tissue paper, napkins, construction paper, etc.

● ■ ▲ 1-2-3 BUBBLE PRINTS

Do this craft in the kitchen sink because it can get messy.

You need:
→ 1 spoonful liquid dish detergent
→ 2 spoonfuls washable, liquid paint (poster paint)
→ 3 spoonfuls warm water
→ Small, shallow bowl (cereal bowl)
→ Drinking straw
→ White paper plate
→ Masking tape

You and child do:
Gently mix detergent, paint, and water in the bowl until smooth.

Measure about seven inches of masking tape and make a loop, sticky side out. Stick this loop to the center of the paper plate, as shown. This will serve as a handle for your "printer."

You do:
Place one end of the straw in the soap-paint solution and gently blow until bubbles mound up over the top of the bowl.

Child does:
Lowers paper plate onto bubbles to print.

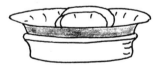

Note:
Your print may look light at first, but after a few minutes the colors get brighter.

Variations:
• Prepare two or three bowls of soap-paint solution and make a multicolored print.
• If paper plates are unavailable, simply lay a sheet of white paper over the bubbles and lift.
• To hang prints, punch a hole along edge of plate and thread with a loop of yarn.

1-2-3 Bubble Prints

■ ▲ PRINTING FROM A PRINTING PLATE

You need:
→ Corrugated cardboard box
→ Lightweight cardboard (cereal or other uncoated food boxes are a good source)
→ Scissors
→ White glue, paste, clear tape, or double-sided tape
→ Liquid paint and paintbrush
→ Paper towel
→ Paper
→ Rolling pin, straight-sided glass, or cardboard tube from paper towels

You do: Cut a flat section from the cardboard box, 5 × 5 inches or larger.

You and child do: Help child cut shapes, 1 × 1-inch or larger, from the lightweight cardboard. Use glue, paste, or loops of tape to attach the shapes to the cardboard piece. Shapes can be applied randomly, or in a design. Allow glue or paste to dry. This is your *printing plate*.

Use paintbrush or fingers to paint the shapes on the printing plate. A sloppy job is fine. (Some children will want to cover the entire printing plate with paint. This is fine too. You'll just get a paintier print.)

When all shapes are painted, lay paper over printing plate and roll gently and evenly with rolling pin, glass, or cardboard tube. Lift paper to reveal print.

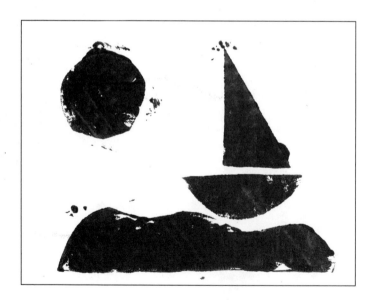

Notes:
- If print comes out smeared, you used too much paint. Just print again, on a new piece of paper.
- Beginner printers may want to start out with only one or two shapes taped or glued to the cardboard background.

Variations: Try attaching different things to the printing plate, like pennies, pipe cleaners, heavily textured wallpaper, etc. If printing especially bumpy and uneven items, print onto a white paper towel instead of regular paper. Lay the paper towel over the printing plate and press gently with hands, rolling pin, or cardboard tube—whichever works best.

● ■ ▲ SPONGE PAINT AND PRINT

You need:
- → Clean sponge
- → Water
- → Liquid paint and paintbrush
- → Paper
- → Rolling pin or straight-sided glass (optional)

You do: Wet the sponge and then squeeze until it's as dry as possible.

Child does: Uses brush, fingers, or cotton swabs to paint directly onto damp sponge. Painting can be a simple picture or pattern, random splotches of color, or child may want to cover entire sponge with paint. Try not to apply paint too thickly! A little goes a long way.

You and child do: Turn sponge paint side down onto paper. Press with hands or roll gently with rolling pin or glass. Lift sponge to see print. Depending on the amount of paint applied, the sponge will print over and over again.

 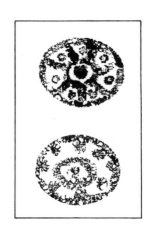

<table>
<tr><td>To reuse sponge:</td><td>When child is ready to change design and colors, wash sponge with dish detergent and warm water, rinse well, squeeze out, and start again.</td></tr>
<tr><td>Markers variation:</td><td>Make fast and easy sponge prints by drawing on a damp sponge with washable markers and then printing as described previously. The best news is that this is a great way to use up all those almost-dried-up markers!</td></tr>
</table>

■ ▲ STYROFOAM PRINT PLATE

You need:
- ➡ Clean Styrofoam meat or vegetable tray, with the edges trimmed off
- ➡ Paintbrush
- ➡ Liquid paint
- ➡ Paper
- ➡ Rolling pin, straight-sided glass, or cardboard tube from paper towels (optional)
- ➡ Crayons (optional)
- ➡ Chopstick (optional)

You and child do:

Use a chopstick or the end of the paintbrush handle to carve a picture or design in the Styrofoam tray. Don't carve all the way through the tray, but try to make your design clearly indented in the Styrofoam. You can also use the tip of the paintbrush handle or chopstick to poke holes in the tray.

Use the paintbrush to cover the surface of the tray lightly with paint. Just paint right over your carved pattern.

Lay paper over the painted tray and roll gently with the cardboard tube, rolling pin, or glass. (You can also press gently with your fingers.) Peel paper up to reveal print.

Variation: Some children prefer to use a dull crayon to draw a picture or design in the Styrofoam tray, pressing hard to make indentations in the Styrofoam. Paint and print as described previously. (If necessary, adults may want to use a paintbrush handle or chopstick to deepen the crayon indentations, before printing.)

See also: Wash, dry, and save your styrofoam print plate to use when making a "Foil Impressions Picture" (page 135).

● ■ ▲ FOIL PRINT

You need:
- ➡ Aluminum foil
- ➡ Scissors
- ➡ White paper
- ➡ Tape
- ➡ Liquid paint
- ➡ Paintbrush (optional)
- ➡ Washable markers (optional)
- ➡ Paper towels

You do: Cut a square of aluminum foil, approximately 5 × 5 inches, and tape it, shiny side up, to a piece of paper. Be sure to tape all sides.

Child does: Uses paintbrush or fingers to paint a simple, colorful picture on foil. Try not to use too much paint, or print will be "smeary."

You and   As soon as foil picture is finished, lay a piece of white
child do: paper over the foil and rub gently to transfer picture.

Child does: Lifts paper to reveal print.

You do: Use dry paper towel to rub foil clean, so child can paint a
new picture and print again.

Washable   Some children prefer to use washable markers instead of
markers   paint. Be sure the markers are fresh and full of color, and
variation: remind child that the markers will smear easily on the
foil. Once the drawing is finished, print immediately,
before the drawing dries.

See also: "Foil Impressions Picture" (page 135).

● ■ ▲ HIDEAWAY PICTURE

You need: ➡ White paper
➡ Scissors
➡ Pencil or crayon
➡ Clear tape
➡ Liquid paints and paintbrush
➡ Sponge pieces

You do: Cut out three to five white paper shapes and tape them, as shown, to a second sheet of white paper. Lift each shape and draw a small, secret picture or message underneath, as shown.

Child does: Without peeking under the paper shapes, child uses technique from "Sponge Paint and Print" (page 110) to cover the entire sheet of paper *and* the paper shapes with colorful sponge prints. When page is completely covered with prints, the paper shapes should be well camouflaged and hard to find!

While the painting is still wet, let your child search for each shape, lift it up, and find your secret hideaway picture or message!

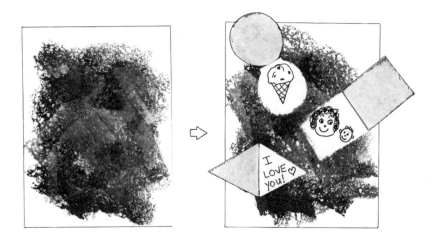

Note: As the painting dries, the paper shapes sometimes tend to curl up, revealing the hideaway pictures. You may want to warn your child about this ahead of time!

8

PLAYING WITH CLAY

One of the nicest things about playing with clay is its versatility. You can poke it, roll it, smoosh it, smash it, pull it apart, mash it together, and, of course, you can make things with it. See "Drying and Baking Instructions" (page 118) for all three of the following recipes.

● ■ ▲ EASY DOUGH

This soft and pliable dough is extra easy to make, with no cooking involved.

You need:
- ➡ $^3/_4$ cup white flour
- ➡ $^1/_2$ cup salt
- ➡ $^1/_2$ cup cornstarch
- ➡ $^2/_3$ cup warm water
- ➡ Mixing bowl
- ➡ Spoon
- ➡ Food colors (optional)

You and child do: Mix all dry ingredients. Add water and stir until mixture comes together. Dust work surface with a little cornstarch and knead dough until smooth. If dough is too sticky, add more cornstarch. If it's too dry, add a little more water.

Notes:
- If desired, add a few drops of food color to the mix as you stir in the water.
- Store dough in a plastic bag. Refrigerate if storing dough for more than a day or two. (Try to allow time for cold dough to return to room temperature, or knead small pieces vigorously, to warm it up before playing.)

● ■ ▲ CORNSTARCH CLAY

This makes a soft, white clay with a wonderfully silky texture.

You need:
- ➡ Saucepan
- ➡ Metal spoon for stirring
- ➡ $^1/_2$ cup cornstarch
- ➡ 1 cup baking soda
- ➡ $^3/_4$ cup plus 2 tablespoons water
- ➡ Dinner plate
- ➡ Paper towel
- ➡ Food colors (optional)

You and child do: ! Combine all ingredients in saucepan. Stir constantly over medium heat. Mixture will foam and then thicken as it comes to a boil. When mixture is the consistency of mashed potatoes and pulls away from bottom of pot, remove from heat.

116

Dump clay onto plate, cover with a wet paper towel, and allow to cool.

When cool, knead clay on work surface dusted with cornstarch. If clay is too sticky, add more cornstarch and knead until clay is silky smooth.

Notes:
- Food coloring can be added during cooking or kneading.
- Air drying is *not recommended* with this clay. (It cracks.)
- Clay can be painted when dry.
- Store clay in a plastic bag. Refrigerate if storing clay for more than a day or two. (Try to allow time for cold clay to return to room temperature, or knead small pieces vigorously, to warm it up before playing.)

● ■ ▲ SPARKLE CLAY

This makes a very gritty, white clay that dries without cracking and has a sparkly finish.

You need:
- ➡ $1/2$ cup cornstarch
- ➡ 1 cup salt
- ➡ $2/3$ cup water
- ➡ Small mixing bowl
- ➡ Saucepan
- ➡ Metal spoon for stirring
- ➡ Dinner plate
- ➡ Paper towel

You and child do:

!

Mix cornstarch and $1/3$ cup water in mixing bowl and set aside.

Mix salt and $1/3$ cup water in saucepan and bring to a boil over medium heat. Lower heat a bit and add the cornstarch liquid to the salty water. Mixture will thicken rapidly and pull away from sides of pot. When clay gathers as a lump on the spoon, remove from heat.

Dump clay on plate, cover with a damp paper towel, and allow to cool.

Dust work surface with cornstarch and knead clay, adding more cornstarch if clay feels too sticky.

Notes:
- If desired, add food coloring to salty water.
- Store clay in a plastic bag. Refrigerate if storing clay for more than a day or two. (Try to allow time for cold

117

clay to return to room temperature, or knead small pieces vigorously, to warm it up before playing.)
- Clay can be painted when dry.

● ■ ▲ DRYING AND BAKING INSTRUCTIONS

*Use these instructions as a general guide for hardening dough and clay creations. However, **watch carefully** since ovens vary in power and temperature, and baking times may be shortened. Microwaving on a Styrofoam grocery tray is the recommended drying technique, since it's easy, fast, and keeps cracking to a minimum.*

Microwave. Place clay pieces on a Styrofoam grocery tray, wax paper, or paper towel. (Shapes won't stick to grocery tray.) For small items, flat shapes, or beads, microwave on High for 45 to 60 seconds. Check pieces for hardness. If possible, turn clay pieces over. Continue to bake for 30 seconds at a time, checking for hardness. Shapes may puff slightly as they bake.

For larger items, microwave for 1 minute, test for hardness, microwave for another minute, and test for hardness again. If possible or practical, turn clay pieces over. Continue to bake for 30 seconds at a time until pieces are hard or almost hard.

Conventional Oven. Place clay pieces on cookie sheet that has been lined with aluminum foil. Bake in a 250°F oven, turning pieces over halfway through baking time:

- Beads, flat shapes, small pieces: 45 to 60 minutes, checking every 15 minutes for hardness or browning.
- Large creations, bowls, etc.: 1 to 2 hours, checking frequently after first 45 minutes. If possible, invert pieces so bottoms can bake.

Air Drying. Air drying is not recommended since it takes so long, and often results in cracked clay. If desired, pieces may be partially dried in microwave, and left to air dry after that.

Air drying "Cornstarch Clay" creations is *not recommended,* since the clay cracks a great deal.

● POKE IT AND SQUASH IT

A first-time activity with clay.

You need:
➥ A small amount of soft dough or clay (See clay recipes at the beginning of this chapter.)

You and child do:
Start with a lump of clay or dough a little bigger than a golf ball. Let your child feel it, poke it, hold it, and squeeze it. Flatten the clay on the work surface and show your child how to poke holes in it with a fingertip. Mold the clay into a small, thin tower, and show your child how to squash it down.

Note:
A great way to introduce your child to clay play is to play with clay yourself. You and your child will have fun sitting together smashing and rolling clay, imitating each other's ideas. For adults who occasionally bake bread, biscuits, or pie crusts, this is the perfect time to hand your child a piece of dough to knead, bake, and eat!

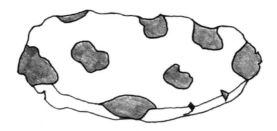

● ■ ▲ WORMS AND SNAKES, CIRCLES AND SHAPES

You need:
➥ Clay or dough (See clay recipes at the beginning of this chapter.)

You and child do:
Start with a walnut-size lump of clay or dough. Show your child how to roll the clay back and forth on the work surface, using a flat hand, until it forms a fat tube. Keep rolling and the tube gets thinner and longer, becoming a snake or worm!

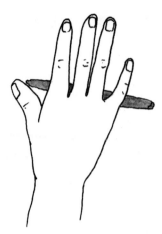

Use an assortment of snakes or worms to create circles, triangles, and other simple shapes. Older children may want to form letters of the alphabet or numbers, spell their names, or even make a happy face or rainbow, if colored clay is available.

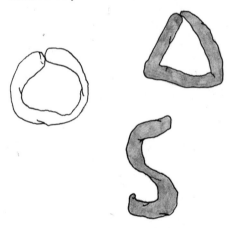

● ■ HAVE A BALL

You need: Clay or dough (See clay recipes at the beginning of this chapter.)

You and child do: Divide clay into marble-size lumps. Show your child how you roll the clay between your palms to form a ball.

Make a collection of clay balls. Ask your child to arrange the balls in a straight line. Then make a circle of balls. Suggest other "clay ball sculptures" such as a pyramid of balls, a tower of balls, or even a clay snowman. Using your hand or the bottom of a glass, show your child how to flatten a clay ball to make a circle.

● ■ ▲ HAVE A BOWL

You need: ➡ Clay or dough (See clay recipes at the beginning of this chapter.)

You and child do: Help your child create some of these easy bowls.

● *Thumbprint Bowl.* Toddlers like to make this bowl because it's tiny. Roll clay into a marble-size ball. Show child how to push a thumb or fingertip into the ball to make a tiny bowl. (Pushing a pencil eraser into the ball of clay makes a tiny bowl too.)

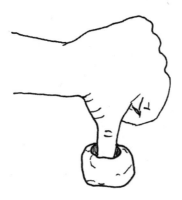

■ *Pinch Bowl.* Roll clay into a ball about the size of a golf ball. Push a thumb into the ball and then, with thumbs on the inside and fingers on the outside, pinch around the edge of the hole until the hole gets bigger and the sides get thinner.

▲ *Coil Bowl.* Flatten a medium-size ball of clay into a circle, about $1/8$ to $1/4$ inch thick and 2 to 3 inches across. Make two or three long "clay snakes" (see page 119). Press a clay snake around the perimeter of the circle. If it isn't long enough, borrow a piece from another snake. Stack a second clay snake on top of the first. If desired, make sides of bowl higher by adding more clay snakes.

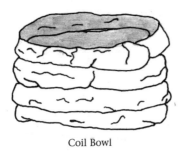

Coil Bowl

● ■ ▲ DRINKING STRAW SCULPTURES

You need:
→ Clay or dough (See clay recipes at the beginning of this chapter.)
→ Plastic drinking straws
→ Wooden toothpicks
→ Scissors

You and child do:
Break toothpicks in half. Cut drinking straws into short lengths, about 1 to 2 inches, depending on the sculpture. Push toothpicks or straws into lumps of clay to create shapes, designs, or creatures. (See "Ideas," below.)

Ideas:
Free-form. Toddlers will have fun pushing straws randomly into lumps of clay. Show child how small lumps of clay can be pushed onto the ends of the straw pieces.

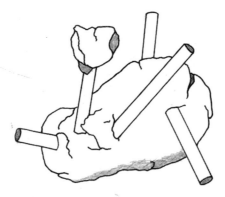

Porcupine. Make a ball of clay the size and shape of an egg, and flatten the bottom on the work surface. Use a pencil point to poke two eyes in one end, or make tiny round eyes from colored clay. Push toothpick pieces into the back of the porcupine to make sharp quills.

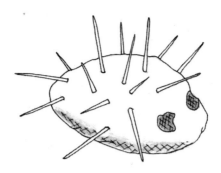

Dragon or Sea Serpent. Roll clay into a long, very fat snake. Decide which end is the head, and either add clay eyes or poke holes for eyes. Roll the tail end slightly thinner. Then push straw pieces into the dragon's or serpent's back for spines. If desired, use scissors or a knife to cut a small mouth and insert toothpicks for scary fangs!

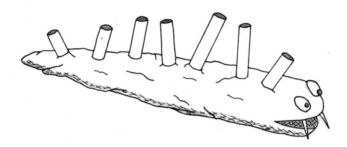

Spider or Octopus. Roll clay into a walnut-size ball, and push eight straw pieces into sides, to form legs. If you're using flexible straws, use the bendable sections for legs, as shown below.

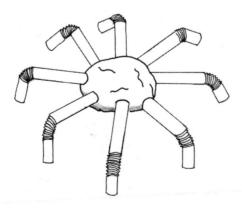

Sea Urchin. Roll clay into a ball. Flatten the bottom on your work surface. Push straw or toothpick pieces into the top and sides.

Space Alien. Make a space alien's head by rolling clay into a ball and pushing two long straw pieces into the top for antennae. Add colored clay, straw sections, or dry beans for alien face details.

Geometric Shapes. Make a collection of small clay balls, a little larger than pea-size. Use the clay balls to connect whole toothpicks, to form two- and three-dimensional shapes, as shown.

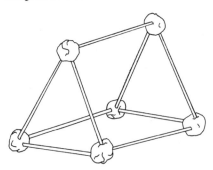

● ■ ▲ ROLL AND CUT

You need:	➡ Clay or dough (See clay recipes at the beginning of this chapter.) ➡ Rolling pin or straight-sided glass ➡ Cookie cutters, plastic knives, pizza cutter (if not too sharp), plastic drinking straws, forks
You and child do:	Start with a lump of clay about the size of a golf ball. Use your hands to flatten the clay, and then roll with the rolling pin or glass until clay is about ¼ inch thick. Use tools and utensils to cut, poke, and make patterns in clay. (See "Ideas," below.)
Ideas:	• Pizza cutters cut nice, clean strips of clay. Have fun cutting clay into straight strips, wavy strips, geometric shapes, or other shapes. Or, make a clay pizza and cut it into wedges! • Use a fork to make a pattern of holes, or press with the back of the fork to make stripes.

- Use a plastic knife to carve clay into shapes. Children may want to practice their fork and knife skills, cutting up pretend clay food! (Be sure to protect your work surface.)
- Cut out cookie cutter shapes. Poke a hole along one edge and bake clay "cookies" until hard (see "Drying and Baking Instructions," page 118). When cool, paint, if desired, and hang up.

- Thread a small cookie cutter or free-form shape on a ribbon or piece of yarn and wear as a necklace.

■ ▲ EASY BEADS

You need:
➡ Clay or dough (See clay recipes at the beginning of this chapter.)
➡ Plastic drinking straws
➡ Wax paper or aluminum foil
➡ Microwave or conventional oven
➡ Poster paints or washable markers (optional)

You and child do:
Roll clay into lots of tiny balls, about the size of very small marbles. Push no more than six balls onto a plastic drinking straw, as shown, making sure balls do not touch each other.

!

Place on wax paper in the microwave, and bake on High for 45 to 60 seconds. Rotate straw to turn beads over, and bake for 30 seconds. Check for hardness and bake for another 30 seconds if needed. If you are baking only one or two beads, baking time may be shorter.

!

To bake beads in a conventional oven, place the clay balls on a foil-lined baking sheet, and use a drinking straw to punch a hole in each ball. *Do not leave drinking straw in beads.* Bake in a 250°F oven for 45 minutes to 1 hour. Test for hardness.

When beads are baked and hard, paint with poster paints or color with markers, if desired.

9
CREATIVE CREATIONS

These three-dimensional projects use skills learned elsewhere in this book and give kids a chance to create something unusual and new. Be sure children understand that there's no one "right" way to do these crafts. The most important idea is to use lots of imagination and to have fun.

■ ▲ COTTON SWAB CONSTRUCTIONS

You need:
➡ Cotton swabs
➡ White glue
➡ Small piece of aluminum foil
➡ Construction paper
➡ Washable markers or paints (optional)

You do: Pour a puddle of white glue onto the aluminum foil.

You and child do: Dip each end of a cotton swab in glue and press it onto the construction paper. Continue adding cotton swabs randomly or in a design.

Variations and ideas: *Color or Paint.* When glue has dried, add color with tempera paints or colored markers. Child can paint swab ends only, the entire swab, or color directly on the background paper.

End-to-End. Position swabs on the paper so that ends are touching, in a variety of patterns.

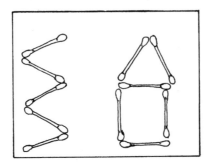

Sunburst. Glue cotton swabs to a colored background (black is especially nice) with swabs meeting at center. Paint, if desired.

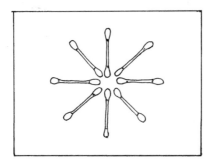

Swab ABCs. Use whole and broken cotton swabs to form letters of the alphabet. Child can create random letters, or spell his or her own name.

Pyramid. Make either a triangular or square pyramid base by gluing three or four cotton swabs to construction paper. Then, dip the ends of three (or four) more cotton swabs in glue and add to base, as shown, to create a pyramid shape. When glue dries, paint cotton swabs, if desired.

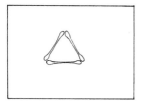 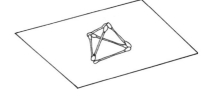

■ ▲ POPSICLE STICK COLLAGE

You need:
→ Collection of wooden Popsicle sticks (from frozen treats or available in bulk at craft stores)
→ Construction paper
→ White glue
→ Washable markers, liquid paint, or crayons

You and child do: This craft sometimes works best if the adult squeezes the glue either onto the paper or the Popsicle sticks, and the child positions the sticks on the paper. Glue sticks randomly, side by side, zigzag, or make shapes or letters. Allow glue to dry, and then color sticks with markers, liquid paint, or crayons.

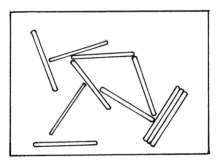

▲ PASTA AND BEAN COLLAGE

You need:
➡ Dry pasta, beans, grains, or other food items that look interesting
➡ Construction paper
➡ White glue

You and child do:
Glue pasta shapes, beans, seeds, grains, or other dry food items to paper to make a free-form design (1). Older children may want to glue down spaghetti or linguine pieces to outline a shape and then fill the inside with grains or beans, as shown (2). Or use different shapes of pasta and beans to create a picture (3).

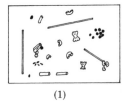

(1)

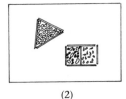

(2)

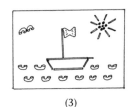

(3)

■ ▲ RAINBOW CRAYONS

This is a great project that uses up lots of broken and stubby crayons!

You need:
→ Broken crayon pieces (all colors)
→ Muffin tin
→ Aluminum foil

You do: Preheat oven to 300°F. Line each muffin cup with foil.

Child does: Peels paper off crayon pieces. If any of your crayon pieces are too big for the muffin cups, ask your child to break them. Then fill each muffin cup about half full of crayon pieces. Encourage your child to choose a wide selection of colors, dark and light, dull and bright, for each cup. Try to have a few more light and bright crayons than dark ones.

! You and child do: Put muffin tin in preheated oven and bake for about 5 to 7 minutes. Watch them *carefully,* because they melt quickly. Try not to let them melt completely—just enough to blend them together.

You do: Carefully remove the crayons from the oven, and let them cool completely, in the muffin tin, for about 30 minutes. Be careful not to shake or bump the tin during cooling time.

Note: At this point, the crayons often look dark and dull on top. Don't despair! The crayons will be prettier and brighter when you peel off the foil.

Child does: When crayons are completely cool, your child can pop each crayon out of the tin and peel off the foil. Each crayon will be different.

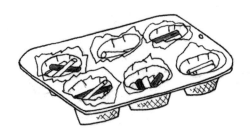

You need: ➡ Colorful crayon shavings from a sharpener
➡ Wax paper (or plain white paper, if wax paper is unavailable)
➡ Newspaper
➡ Iron
➡ Scissors
➡ Clear tape

You and child do: Layer a few sheets of newspaper over the ironing surface. Lay a sheet of wax paper on the newspaper, and sprinkle lightly with brightly colored crayon shavings. Cover with a second sheet of wax paper, and one more piece of newspaper.

! You do: Iron with a warm iron for 2 to 3 seconds, until crayon shavings melt.

Child does: Cuts colorful wax paper into desired shape and tapes in a sunny window.

Plain Paper Sparklers. Repeat preceding directions, using lightweight, plain white paper instead of wax paper. You will have to iron a bit longer for crayon shavings to melt completely. These Plain Paper Sparklers look rather dull until you hold them up to the light and they glow with color!

● ■ ▲ STYROFOAM SWIRL JEWELRY

You need:
➡ Styrofoam grocery tray (washed carefully and dried)
➡ Scissors
➡ Washable markers
➡ White glue
➡ Microwave oven
➡ Toothpick or sharp pencil
➡ Yarn

You and child do: Cut grocery tray into shapes about 1 to 2 inches across. Color each shape with splotches of two, three, or four marker colors (1). While marker is still wet, spread a layer of white glue over the surface, swirling the colors with your finger (2). Allow to air dry, or dry in microwave (see below).

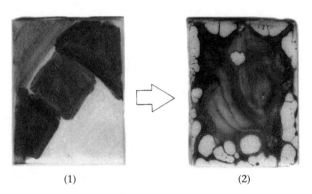

(1)   (2)

When glue is completely dry and hard, use a toothpick or pencil point to poke a hole in the shape, thread with yarn, and wear as jewelry.

To dry in microwave: Drying shapes in the microwave makes the finish shiny! After spreading with glue, place Styrofoam pieces on a paper towel. Microwave on High for 1 to 3 minutes, with 2 cups of water in the oven.

!   *Watch carefully.* When glue no longer looks white, it is dry.

Note: On certain types of Styrofoam, the swirled glue will shrink away from the edges while drying. There are two things you can do if this happens. You can keep the jewelry piece as it is, if you like the effect. Or you can cut an extra large piece of Styrofoam to begin with (3 inches across), swirl the colors on that, dry it, and then cut out your desired shape from the center.

Crayon variation: Follow the preceding directions except color with crayons instead of markers. The crayon colors will not swirl, but the result is very colorful and pretty!

■ ▲ PICTURE SEWING CARDS

This is a very portable, non-messy toy for in the car!

You need:
- Lightweight cardboard (poster board, backs of notepads, cardboard from tights or stockings, manila folders)
- Markers or crayons
- Paper punch
- Yarn (2 to 3 feet long)
- Clear tape
- Clear self-adhesive vinyl paper

You *or* child do: Either you or your child can draw the pictures for these sewing cards. If your child prefers an adult-type drawing, that's fine. If your child prefers his or her own work, that's fine too. A compromise might be your drawing on one side of the card and your child's drawing on the other side. Whatever you decide, try to keep the drawings simple.

You do: Cover both sides of card with clear, self-adhesive vinyl, and punch holes in the drawing. If the picture has obvious corners, punch holes there. If not, simply punch five to ten holes at random.

Note: If your sewing card has a drawing on both sides, remember that the holes will match the corners of one drawing, but not the other.

You do: Tie one end of yarn through a hole near the edge of the cardboard. Wrap a bit of tape around the other end of the yarn, to make threading easier.

Child does: Sews in and out of holes, following lines of the drawing, or sewing randomly.

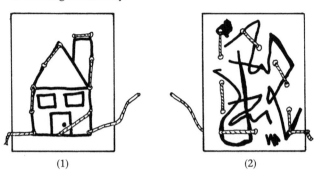

(1)   (2)

▲ FOIL IMPRESSIONS PICTURE

You need: ➡ Styrofoam grocery tray
➡ Scissors
➡ Pencil, knitting needle, chopstick, or paintbrush
➡ Aluminum foil
➡ Construction paper
➡ Masking tape

You and child do: Cut curved edges off Styrofoam grocery tray. Use a dull pencil, a knitting needle, chopstick, or the end of a paintbrush handle to carve a picture or design into the Styrofoam tray (1). (See "Styrofoam Print Plate," page 111.) Cover the tray with a piece of aluminum foil, shiny side down. Use your fingers to press and rub the foil into the carved design. Lift foil. Mount foil picture, shiny side up, on construction paper, using masking tape as a frame (2).

(1)   (2)

Variations:
- Younger children may find it easier to use a dull crayon to draw a picture or design in the Styrofoam tray. Then an adult can go over drawing with a sharper implement to deepen the crayon indentations.
- See "Printing from a Printing Plate" (page 108) for another way to make a textured picture. Press foil against the printing plate and rub with fingers until design or picture appears.

▲ FANCY HATS

You need:
- ➡ Disposable 9- or 10-inch plates (paper or plastic)
- ➡ Scissors
- ➡ Pencil, markers, crayons
- ➡ Gift ribbon, yarn, construction paper, pipe cleaners, recyclables
- ➡ Clear tape

You and child do: From the inside of paper plates, cut out the patterns shown below to create a crown, wings, or floppy ears. (For winged hat, cut out and discard the shaded areas.) Wear the hats so the plate brim points down.

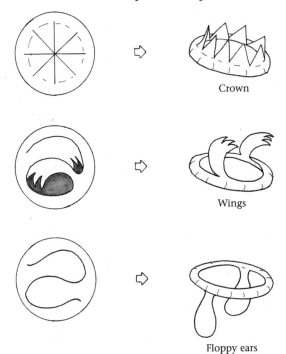

Crown

Wings

Floppy ears

Another hat technique is to cut out the center of a paper plate, so that the plate fits your child's head. Then color the remaining circle with markers or crayons, and attach ribbon, yarn, paper flowers, pipe cleaners, etc. to drip over the edge of the hat.

▲ PAPER PLATE NOTE HOLDER

You need:
➡ Two white paper plates
➡ Scissors
➡ Crayons or washable markers
➡ Two or three paper clips
➡ Paper punch
➡ Three feet of yarn
➡ Masking tape

Child does:
Draws a colorful design or picture on the eating surface of one white paper plate (1).

Cuts the second paper plate in half, and draws a design or picture on the *underside* surface of one of the half-plates (2).

(1)

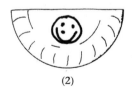

(2)

You and child do:
Place the half-plate, picture side up, over the bigger picture. Flatten the half-plate against the picture, edges even, and use paper clips to hold it in place.

137

You do: Punch holes through both plates, as shown.

You and   Wrap a bit of tape around one end of the yarn (to make
child do: sewing easier) and sew the two plates together, using an
                overhand stitch, an in-and-out stitch, or a combination
                of the two. Then pop the half-plate back out, forming a
                space for mail, notes, or special surprises. Punch a hole in
                the top of the first plate, to hang it up.

■ ▲ SOAP CARVING

A fun and easy sculpting experience.

You need: ➡ A *fresh* bar of Ivory soap (to ensure softness and no
                  splitting)
                ➡ Pencil
                ➡ Teaspoon
                ➡ Butter knife
                ➡ Sharp knife (for adult use only)
                ➡ Plastic drinking straws, clear tape, scissors, paper,
                  toothpicks, dry pasta

Notes: Be sure to use very fresh soap. The soap should have a creamy texture that doesn't split or splinter when you cut or carve it. If a large piece does break while you're carving, you can "glue" it back together by wetting one surface with water, fitting the pieces together, and letting it dry.

You and child do: Use the butter knife and spoon to carve shapes in the soap, and use the pencil point to carve details. Once your child decides what to carve (see "Ideas"), you can draw a rough design or guide right on the bar of soap. Any small mistakes can be erased by rubbing the soap with a wet finger. Any large mistakes can simply be cut off, so you can start again.

Ideas: *Boat.* Cut off two end corners of a bar of Ivory soap (1). Then scoop out the center of the soap, being careful not to scoop through the bottom (2). Push a toothpick or a piece of drinking straw into the back of the boat and attach a paper sail with tape (3).

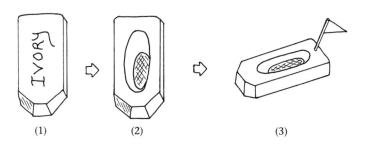

(1)   (2)   (3)

Raft. Use a sharp knife to cut a bar of Ivory soap into three or four long pieces. Cut plastic drinking straws into $1\frac{1}{2}$-inch lengths. Push the straw sections into the cut edges of the soap, to create a raft, as shown.

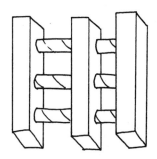

Face. Carve out holes for eyes and press a small piece of drinking straw into the center of each hole. Use toothpick or drinking straw pieces for hair, and a macaroni elbow for a nose.

Car. Use a pencil point to sketch a car shape on the side of a fresh bar of soap (1). Carve the soap into the car shape with a butter knife, smoothing soap edges. Use the knife to shave off any logo on the side of the soap, and sketch window and door details with a pencil (2). Cut wheels out of construction paper or Styrofoam trays, and attach to the car with toothpick pieces. Add a toothpick for an antenna (3).

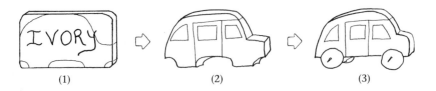

(1)   (2)   (3)

Animals. Make a pencil sketch on the side and top of the soap, and use a sharp knife to carve out a general animal shape. Shave off the soap logo with a butter knife. Then ask your child to think up some important details about the animal. Add drinking straws, toothpicks, or pasta pieces for horns, quills, or spines. Paper details such as ears or wings can be added by cutting slits in the soap with a sharp knife. Insert paper cutouts into the slits. Sketch in fur with a pencil point.

This is a great way to reuse Styrofoam trays!

You need:
- ➡ Styrofoam grocery trays (carefully washed, rinsed, and dried)
- ➡ Scissors
- ➡ Knitting needle, pencil, and/or teaspoon
- ➡ Crayons, washable markers, or permanent markers (optional)
- ➡ Plastic drinking straw
- ➡ Clear tape

Styrofoam tray hints:
- *Number of trays*—The size of your construction depends on the number of trays you have, so plan ahead. It's good to have at least one extra tray, in case of mistakes.
- *Cutting*—Styrofoam trays cut easily with scissors. You can also use a knitting needle or pencil point to carve your design into the tray, carving deeper and deeper until you cut through. Tabs (top edge of the "Castle," for instance) snap off if you cut each side and bend the tab down. To cut curves or wavy lines, press the curved edge of a teaspoon into the tray.
- *Color*—Crayons color Styrofoam trays beautifully. You can also use permanent or washable markers, although washable markers will smear a bit before they dry.
- *Fitting pieces together*—Put your sculpture together by cutting 1/4- to 1/2-inch long slits in connecting pieces. The slits are made by making two small cuts, very close together, and removing the sliver of Styrofoam. If the Styrofoam tray feels a little too fat to fit in the slit, simply squeeze the uncut Styrofoam to make it thinner, or widen the slit a bit.

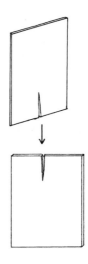

A second way to fit some pieces together (the "Castle" or "Horse Corral," for example) is with clear tape.

You and child do: Cut curved edges off trays. Draw your desired shapes directly on the Styrofoam tray (see "Ideas" below), and cut them out using any of the methods described previously. *Color the shapes before putting the sculpture together.* Because these will be three-dimensional sculptures, be sure to color both sides of the Styrofoam pieces.

Ideas: *Free-form.* Cut trays into squares, triangles, and rectangles, each at least 2 inches across. Color shapes, if desired. Cut two, three, or four slits in each piece, as shown. Slits can be anywhere from $1/2$ inch to 1 inch long. Fit pieces together to make free-form constructions.

Horse Corral, Fence, or Fort. Decide how large or small your corral, fence, or fort will be, and cut pieces accordingly. Five or six 2×8-inch pieces will make a big corral. Five or six 2×4-inch pieces will make a small corral. Color, if desired, cut slits as shown, and fit together. For a fancier corral, cut out the center of each piece, as shown, and color Styrofoam brown, so pieces resemble logs or boards. For a faster corral, tape the pieces together instead of cutting slits.

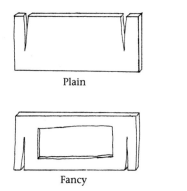

Plain

Fancy

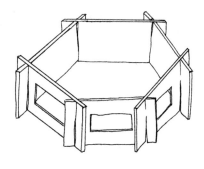

Animals and Creatures. Decide on your animal ahead
of time, or make one up as you go along. Draw an
outline of the head, neck, body, and tail, as shown, and
cut it out. Cut out leg and foot pieces, and ears or
horns. Color both sides of all pieces. Cut slits as shown
below.

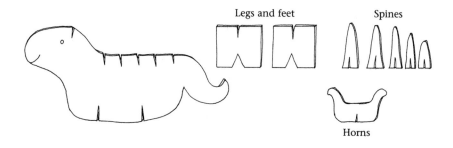

Legs and feet

Spines

Horns

Fit the pieces together to create your three-
dimensional creature. Your child can then decide on
additional features to add: spines, bigger ears, longer tail.
If creature falls forward, either trim back feet to be lower,
bend front legs slightly forward, or add a longer tail.

People. Draw an outline of person's head and torso. Draw two arm and hand sections and two leg and foot sections. Cut out the shapes and color on both sides. Cut slits, as shown, and fit pieces together. If person tips over when you stand it up, simply trim bottom of feet with scissors to slant forward or backward.

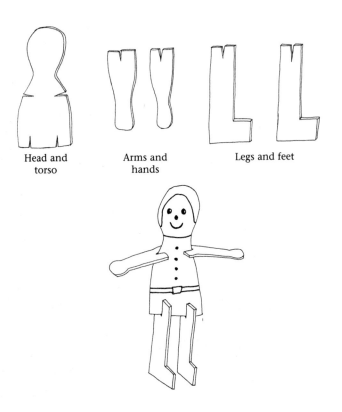

Head and
torso

Arms and
hands

Legs and feet

Castle. You need at least two trays to make a castle. Cut each tray in half, and make ¹/₂-inch-long cuts along the top edge of each piece. Snap off every other tab.

Use scissors to cut windows and doors in walls. A sharp pencil works well to poke peep holes. Color walls, draw a stone or brick pattern, or leave plain. *Decorate only one side of each piece.*

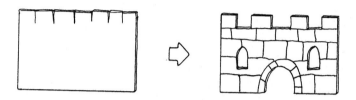

Use clear tape to stick the walls together. Place wall pieces colored sides *down*. With edges tightly together, tape seams. Also tape one remaining edge, as shown.

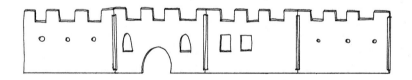

Form taped walls into a square shape, taping last seam on inside. Make flags from scraps of Styrofoam, colored and taped to inside walls. Add additional buildings and towers, if desired.

Other Ideas: Encourage your child to think up more creative projects. Make a car using drinking straw pieces as axles for 3-D tires. Older children may enjoy experimenting with different glider designs.

● ■ ▲ BOX DESK

You need:
→ A sturdy, medium-size box (The size of the box depends on the size of your child.)
→ Pencil or marker
→ Heavyweight scissors or razor knife (for adult use)
→ Duct tape

You do: Turn the box over and use duct tape to reinforce sides and seams, if needed. Draw and cut sections out of the box, as shown in the illustration.

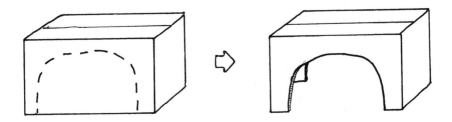

Child does: Sits with legs through box opening, drawing or painting at a small, private desk!

● ■ ▲ ART BOX

This is a fun and exciting project to do together, or surprise your child with an Art Box as a gift!

You need:
➡ Sturdy box with lid (A box that held winter or hiking boots is perfect.)
➡ Colorful self-adhesive vinyl (available in supermarkets or hardware stores)
➡ Art supplies (See "Ideas," below.)

You do: Cover box with self-adhesive vinyl. Fill with art supplies.

Ideas:
• Paper (white, construction, tissue)
• Washable markers, crayons, chalk, pencils
• Pencil/crayon sharpener
• Paint (children's liquid paint, watercolors, fingerpaint)
• Paintbrushes
• Safety scissors
• White glue, paste, glue stick, tape
• Yarn
• Paper towels
• Recycled items (Styrofoam grocery trays, cardboard tubes, etc.)
• Colorful adhesive stickers, glitter

INDEX

●■▲●■▲●■▲●■▲●■▲●■▲●■▲